THE ULTIMATE BREVILLE SMART AIR FRYER OVEN PRO COOKBOOK

HEALTHY, EFFORTLESS, AND DELICIOUS RECIPES + 2 EASY 28 DAYS MEAL PLANS: CLASSIC AND LIGHT FOR ANY OCCASION. CLEAR CHARACTERS, ONE RECIPE FOR PAGE

SEMPLICESAVOR

COPYRIGHT

TABLE OF CONTENT

INTRODUCTION 9

Welcome to the Breville Smart Air Fryer Oven Pro Cookbook! 9

HOW TO USE BREVILLE SMART AIR FRYER OVEN PRO 10

CLEANING AND MAINTENANCE OF BREVILLE SMART AIR FRYER OVEN PRO 11

BREAKFAST RECIPES 12

1. Banana Pancakes 12
2. Apple and Cinnamon Muffins 13
3. Bacon and Cheese Omelet 14
4. Oatmeal and honey pancakes 15
5. Waffles with Maple Syrup 16
6. Nutella Crepes 17
7. Banana and Chocolate Porridge 18
8. French Toast 19
9. Omelet with Spinach and Cheese 20
10. Banana and Oatmeal Cheese Pancakes 21

APERITIF SNACK RECIPES 22

11. Bruschette with Sun-Dried Tomatoes and Mozzarella Cheese 22
12. Olive all'ascolana 23
13. Crostini with Liver Pate 24
14. Pinzimonio with Fresh Vegetables and Yogurt Sauce 25
15. Tuna and Potato Meatballs 26
16. Baked Potato Chips 27
17. Arancini with Meat Sauce 28
18. Mini Quiche with Spinach and Cheese 29

FISH AND SEAFOOD RECIPES 30

19. Shrimp and Pineapple Skewers 30
20. Potato and Cheese Croquettes 31
21. Pineapple Cod Fillets 32
22. Pineapple Squid 33
23. Pineapple Coconut Shrimp 34
24. Pineapple Tuna Meatballs 35
25. Pineapple Chicken Wings 36
26. Sea Bass in Pineapple Air Fryer 37
27. Pineapple Sweet Potato Fries 38

28. Pineapple Corn Fritters 39

29. Pineapple Air Fryer Fried Ravioli..40

30. Bananas Falafel 41

31. Baked Salmon with Lemon And Herbs 42

POULTRY RECIPES 43

32. Chicken Hunting...43

33. Chicken's Breast With Lemon 44

34. Roasted Chicken With Potatoes 45

35. Chicken Curry 46

36. Spicy Chicken Wings 47

37. Grilled Chicken With Barbecue Sauce 48

38. Chicken Straccetti with Rucola And Tomatoes...49

39. Baked Chicken With Spices 50

40. Grilled Chicken With Grilled Vegetables..51

41. Chicken With Mushrooms And Panna 52

BEEF AND LAMB RECIPES..53

42. Beef Filet With Green Pepper 53

43. Roast Of Beef With Potatoes 54

44. Skewers of Beef and Vegetables 55

45. Sliced Beef with Rocket and Grana Cheese..56

46. Beef Stew With Vegetables..57

47. Lamb Costolets 58

48. Roast of lamb with rosemary and garlic...59

49. Pizzaiola Meat 60

50. Beef Hamburger with Bacon and Cheese 61

51. Lamb Stew with Carrots And Peas..62

PORK RECIPES...63

52. Pork Roast with Potatoes 63

53. Pork Ribs 64

54. Pork Tenderloin in Bacon Crust..65

55. Skewers of Pigs and Pineapples...66

56. Pork Stew with Mushrooms And Potatoes 67

57. Pigeon Bread with Carrots and Sedanes...68

58. Pork Curry with Based Rice 69

59. Roast Pork with Potatoes and Carrots 70

60. Stewed Pig with Beans 71

61. Pork Ribs with Tomato Salad 72

62. Pork Slices with Senape...73

63. Pork Sausages 74

64. Pork Pulpets with Sugar 75

VEGETABLE AND VEGAN RECIPES...76

65. Grilled Vegetable Tacos...76
66. Sesame tofu...77
67. Vegetable Casserole...78
68. Potato and Spinach Croquettes...79
69. Baked Stuffed Mushrooms Air Fryer...80
70. Artichokes Stuffed...81
71. Kale chips...82
72. Chickpea and Sweet Potato Meatballs...83
73. Vegetarian Chili with Beans and Corn...84
74. Vegetarian Lasagna with Spinach and Ricotta Cheese...85
75. Quinoa and Lentil Burger...86
76. Porcini Mushroom Risotto...87
77. Savory Pie with Zucchini and Carrots...88

SANDWICHES AND PIZZA RECIPES...89

78. Ham and Mozzarella Cheese Sandwich...89
79. Tuna and Sun-Dried Tomato Sandwich...90
80. Chicken and Avocado Sandwich...91
81. Focaccia with Cherry Tomatoes and Basil...92
82. Pizza Margherita...93
83. Eggplant and Goat Cheese Sandwich...94
84. Pizza with Mushrooms and Sausage...95
85. Calzone with Ham and Cheese...96
86. Salmon and Arugula Pizza...97
87. Sandwich with Meatballs and Tomato Sauce...98

DESSERT RECIPES...99

88. Air Fryer Oven Strawberry Tiramisu...100
89. Air Fryer Oven Chocolate Cheesecake...101
90. Air Fryer Lemon Doughnut...102
91. Air Fryer Oven Dark Chocolate Brownies...103
92. Air Fryer Oven Banana and Chocolate Muffins...104
93. Air Fryer Oven Catalan Cream with Caramel...105
94. Air Fryer Oven Apple and Cinnamon Crumble...106
95. Air Fryer Oven Chocolate and Hazelnut Cake...107
96. Air Fryer Oven Homemade Vanilla Ice Cream...108
97. Air Fryer Oven Fresh Fruit Tart...109

FESTIVE DISHES...110

98. Croutons with Goat Cheese and Honey...110
99. Smoked Salmon and Avocado Canapés...111
100. Air Fryer Ham and Cheese Puffs...112
101. Air Fryer Oven Meatballs with Mushroom Sauce...113
102. Arancini Pasta with Meat Sauce and Peas...114

103. Salmon Mousse with Spring Onion 115
104. Gnocchi with Gorgonzola and Walnuts...116
105. Potato and Sausage Flan 117

CLASSIC 28-MEAL PLAN   118
Week 1: 118
Week 2: 118
Week 3: 119
Week 4: 119

LOW-CALORIE 28-MEAL PLAN   120
Week 1: 120
Week 2: 120
Week 3: 121
Week 4: 121

CONCLUSION   122
BONUS 123

INDEX   124

INTRODUCTION

Welcome to the Breville Smart Air Fryer Oven Pro Cookbook!

The Breville Smart Air Fryer Oven Pro is the newest addition to the Breville line of small kitchen appliances. The Air Fryer Pro is designed to fry food with little to no oil by using rapid hot air circulation, ensuring even and efficient cooking. Additionally, it features a dehydration function for making dried fruits and vegetables, as well as a bake function suitable for cookies, cakes, cheesecakes, muffins, cupcakes, and other desserts.

This smart kitchen appliance cooks food in a special chamber using super-heated air, facilitated by a convection mechanism, which ensures even cooking from all sides.

The Breville Smart Air Fryer Oven Pro comes with a variety of accessories, including a pizza pan, two oven racks, a broil rack, a roasting pan, an air fryer basket, a baking pan, and a dehydrator tray. Whether you're baking, air frying, roasting, broiling, or dehydrating, this oven can do it all.

Before the first use, ensure to remove and discard any packaging material, labels, and tape from the unit, as well as all accessories. Rinse the basket, wire rack, sheet pan, and crumb tray with hot soapy water, followed by a rinse under clean water and thorough drying. Note that only the basket, sheet pan, crumb tray, and wire rack are dishwasher-safe; the main unit should never be cleaned in the dishwasher.

Benefits of the Breville Smart Air Fryer Oven Pro:

- Versatile cooking options: air fry, broil, bake, toast, and warm.
- Easy preparation of various meals, including chicken roast, beef, leg of lamb, fresh and frozen vegetables, fruits, desserts, snacks, appetizers, and more.
- Simple cleaning process with step-by-step instructions provided. Avoid using harsh chemicals to prevent damage to the equipment.
- Multiple cooking modes available: air fry, broil, bake, convection bake, and dehydrate.

With its array of features and capabilities, the Breville Smart Air Fryer Oven Pro is an ideal choice for anyone seeking a versatile and convenient kitchen appliance.

HOW TO USE BREVILLE SMART AIR FRYER OVEN PRO

Breville Smart Air Fryer Oven Pro is a versatile appliance capable of roasting, air frying, baking, broiling, and dehydrating. Here's a step-by-step guide on how to use this air fryer oven:

Preheat the oven by pressing the "preheat" button. The default temperature is set to 400 degrees F. Adjust the temperature using the +/- buttons as needed.

Place the food onto the wire rack included with the appliance. If using the air fryer mode, also insert the air fryer basket into the oven.

Set the cooking time by pressing the "timer" button. The default time is 30 minutes, but you can adjust it using the up or down buttons according to your recipe's instructions.

Once the timer is set, press the "start" button to begin cooking.

When the cooking time is complete, the air fryer oven will automatically stop. If you wish to continue cooking, simply press the "start" button again.

Use tongs to cautiously open the oven door and check the food. Be mindful of hot steam when opening the door.

Once the food is cooked to your liking, remove it from the air fryer oven.

Allow the food to cool for a moment before serving.

With these simple steps, you can make the most of your Breville Smart Air Fryer Oven Pro for delicious and convenient cooking!

CLEANING AND MAINTENANCE OF BREVILLE SMART AIR FRYER OVEN PRO

Everyday Cleaning:

The unit should be thoroughly cleaned after each use. Begin by unplugging the unit from the outlet and allowing it to cool down before cleaning. Empty the racks and wash them by hand when necessary.

If any food splatter is stuck on the interior walls of the unit, clean and wipe them with a damp, soft sponge. Use warm, soapy water for tougher stains. Clean the exterior of the main unit and control panel with a damp cloth. Only use a non-abrasive liquid cleanser or mild spray solution. Apply the solution or cleanser to the sponge, not directly to the oven surface, before cleaning.

Deep Cleaning:

Again, start by unplugging the unit from the outlet and allowing it to cool down. Remove all accessories from the unit, including the crumb tray, and rinse them separately. Use a non-abrasive cleaning brush to rinse the air fryer basket.

To access the interior of the oven, flip it into the storage position and press the button to release the back door. Clean the interior of the oven with warm, soapy water and a soft cloth. Avoid abrasive cleaners, chemical cleaners, or scrubbing brushes as they can damage the oven. Never put the main unit in the dishwasher or immerse it in water or liquid. However, the sheet pan and air fryer basket are dishwasher safe.

Once all accessories are dry, place them back in the oven for future use.

BREAKFAST RECIPES

1. BANANA PANCAKES

Prep + Cook time: 10 min | **Serving:** 2 People

Ingredients:

» 1 ripe banana
» 1 egg
» 1/2 cup flour
» 1 teaspoon baking powder
» 1 pinch of salt
» Olive oil to taste

Preparation:

1. In a bowl, mash the banana with a fork.
2. Add the egg and beat with a whisk.
3. Add the flour, baking powder, and salt and mix until smooth.
4. In a nonstick pan, heat a drizzle of olive oil and pour the mixture by spoonfuls.
5. Bake the pancakes at 180°C for 5-7 minutes per side, until golden brown.
6. Serve pancakes warm with maple syrup or fresh fruit.

Nutrition per portion: Calories: 215 kcal- Protein: 6 g- Fat: 7 g- Carbohydrates: 37 g- Fiber: 3g- Sugars: 7 g.

Remember that these values are based on approximate estimates and may vary depending on specific brands and the quantities of ingredients used; this applies to all recipes.

Use a Ripe Banana: Choose a banana that is ripe as it will mash more easily and provide natural sweetness to the pancakes. A riper banana will also contribute to a softer texture.

Don't Overmix the Batter Mix the ingredients until just combined. Overmixing can result in tough pancakes. It's okay if there are a few lumps in the batter; they will disappear during cooking.

Control the Heat: Use medium heat to cook the pancakes. Too high heat can cause them to brown too quickly on the outside while remaining raw on the inside. Test the temperature by dropping a small amount of batter into the pan; it should sizzle gently.

Remember, practice makes perfect when it comes to pancake-making. Enjoy your delicious breakfast treat!

2. APPLE AND CINNAMON MUFFINS

Prep + Cook time: 30 min | **Serving:** 6 muffins

Ingredients:

- » 1 apple
- » 1 egg
- » 1/2 cup milk
- » 1/4 cup sunflower seed oil
- » 1 cup flour

- » 1/2 cup sugar
- » 2 teaspoons baking powder
- » 1 teaspoon cinnamon powder
- » 1 pinch of salt

Preparation:

1. Peel and cut the apple into cubes.
2. In a bowl, beat the egg, milk, and sunflower oil.
3. Add the flour, sugar, baking powder, cinnamon, and salt, and mix until smooth.
4. Add the apple cubes and mix gently.
5. Pour the mixture into 6 muffin pans and place them in an air oven preheated to 180°C for 18-20 minutes, until they are golden brown and cooked in the center.
6. Take the muffins out of the oven and let them cool before serving.

Nutrition per portion: Calories: 258 kcal- Protein: 3 g- Fat: 10 g- Carbohydrates: 37 g- Fiber: 1,2 g- Sugars: 20 g

Choose the Right Apple: Opt for a firm apple variety like Granny Smith or Fuji that holds its shape well when baked. These varieties also offer a nice balance of sweet and tart flavors, complementing the cinnamon and sugar in the muffins.

Don't Overmix the Batter: Mix the wet and dry ingredients until just combined. Overmixing can lead to dense and tough muffins. It's okay if there are a few small lumps in the batter; they will disappear during baking.

Add a Topping: Before baking, consider sprinkling a mixture of cinnamon and sugar on top of each muffin for added flavor and texture. This will create a delicious crust on the muffins as they bake and add a hint of sweetness to each bite.

3. BACON AND CHEESE OMELET

Prep + Cook time: 15 min | **Serving:** 2 People

Ingredients:

» 4 eggs
» 1/4 cup milk
» 1/4 cup grated cheese

» 50g diced bacon
» Salt and pepper to taste

Preparation:

1. In a bowl, beat the eggs with the milk, grated cheese, salt, and pepper.
2. In a nonstick skillet, cook bacon over medium-low heat for 5-7 minutes, until golden brown and crispy.
3. Pour the egg mixture into the pan with the bacon and cook over medium heat for 5-7 minutes, until the egg is cooked but still soft.
4. Place the skillet in the oven at 180°C for about 3-4 minutes, until the omelet is puffy and golden brown on the surface.
5. Serve the omelet hot and cut into slices.

Nutrition per portion: Calories: 345 kcal- Protein: 25 g- Fat: 26 g- Carbohydrates: 3 g- Fiber: 0 g- Sugars: 2 g

Cook the Bacon First: Start by cooking the diced bacon in the skillet until it's golden brown and crispy. This allows the bacon to release its flavorful fat, which will add richness to the omelet. Plus, pre-cooking the bacon ensures that it's evenly distributed throughout the omelet.

Use Low Heat: When cooking the omelet in the skillet, use medium-low heat. This prevents the eggs from browning too quickly on the bottom while ensuring that they cook through evenly. A slower cooking process also helps maintain a soft and fluffy texture.

Finish in the Oven: After cooking the omelet on the stovetop, transfer the skillet to the oven and broil it for a few minutes. This allows the top of the omelet to puff up and become golden brown, while the cheese melts and becomes gooey. Keep a close eye on the omelet in the oven to prevent it from overcooking.

By following these tips, you'll create a delicious Bacon and Cheese Omelet that's packed with flavor and has a perfect texture. Enjoy your breakfast!

4. OATMEAL AND HONEY PANCAKES

Prep + Cook time: 20 min | **Serving:** 2 People

Ingredients:

- » 1 cup oatmeal
- » 1 ripe banana
- » 2 eggs
- » 2 tablespoons honey
- » 1 teaspoon cinnamon powder
- » 1/4 teaspoon salt
- » Olive oil to taste

Preparation:

1. In a bowl, mash the banana with a fork.
2. Add the eggs, honey, cinnamon, salt, and oatmeal and mix until smooth.
3. In a nonstick skillet, heat a drizzle of olive oil and pour the mixture by spoonfuls.
4. Bake the pancakes in an air oven at 180°C for 10-12 minutes per side, until golden brown.

Nutrition per portion: Calories: 280 kcal- Protein: 9 g- Fat: 11 g- Carbohydrates: 38 g- Fiber: 5 g- Sugars: 11 g

Blend the Oatmeal for a Smoother Batter: Instead of using whole oats, consider blending the oatmeal into a finer texture before mixing it with the other ingredients. This will create a smoother batter, resulting in pancakes with more uniform consistency.

Let the Batter Rest: After mixing all the ingredients, let the batter rest for about 5-10 minutes. This allows the oats to absorb some of the moisture, resulting in thicker and fluffier pancakes.

Cook Slowly for Even Browning: keep a close eye on the pancakes to prevent overcooking and flip them halfway through the baking time for even browning.

By following these tips, you'll achieve perfectly cooked Oatmeal and Honey Pancakes that are both healthy and delicious. Enjoy your meal!

5. WAFFLES WITH MAPLE SYRUP

Prep + Cook time: 20 min | **Serving:** 2 People

Ingredients:

- » 1 cup 00 flour
- » 1/2 cup milk
- » 1 egg
- » 2 tablespoons sugar
- » 1 teaspoon baking powder

- » 1/2 teaspoon baking soda
- » 1/4 teaspoon salt
- » 2 tablespoons melted butter
- » Maple syrup for serving

Preparation:

1. Turn on the oven to 200°C and wait until it reaches temperature.
2. In a bowl, combine the flour, sugar, baking powder, baking soda, and salt.
3. In another bowl, beat the egg and add the milk and melted butter.
4. Pour the liquids into the bowl of dry ingredients and mix until smooth.
5. Pour the mixture into previously buttered and floured air oven ramekins.
6. Close the lid of the air oven and bake the waffles for about 10 to 12 minutes or until golden brown and crispy.
7. Serve the waffles warm with maple syrup to taste.

Nutrition per portion: Calories: 240 kcal- Protein: 6 g- Fat: 9 g- Carbohydrates: 34 g- Fiber: 1 g- Sugars: 8 g

Don't Overmix the Batter: When combining the wet and dry ingredients, mix just until combined. Overmixing can develop the gluten in the flour, making the waffles tough and chewy instead of light and airy.

6. NUTELLA CREPES

Prep + Cook time: 20 min | **Serving:** 2 People

Ingredients:

» 2 eggs
» 1/2 cup 00 flour
» 1/2 cup milk

» 1 pinch of salt
» Nutella for serving

Preparation:

1. Turn on the air oven to 200°C and wait until it reaches temperature.
2. In a bowl, beat the eggs with the flour, milk, and salt until smooth and homogeneous.
3. Pour the mixture into previously buttered and floured air oven ramekins.
4. Bake the crepes for about 5-6 minutes, or until golden brown and cooked through.
5. Serve the crepes warm with a generous portion of Nutella in the center.

Nutrition per portion: Calories: 310 kcal, Protein: 11.5 g, Fat: 12.25 g, Carbohydrates: 37.5 g, Fiber: 0.5 g, Sugars: 16.5 g

Ensure a Smooth Batter: When mixing the eggs, flour, milk, and salt, make sure there are no lumps. You can use a blender or a whisk to achieve a smooth and homogeneous batter. A smooth batter ensures even cooking and a delicate texture.

Properly Grease the Cooking Surface: Before pouring the batter into the air oven ramekins, make sure they are well-buttered and floured. This prevents the crepes from sticking and helps them achieve a golden brown color.

Watch the Cooking Time Carefully: Crepes cook quickly, usually within 5-6 minutes. Keep an eye on them to prevent overcooking, which can make them dry and brittle. They should be golden brown and cooked through but still soft and pliable.

By following these tips, you'll be able to make delicious Nutella crepes that are perfectly cooked and ready to be enjoyed.

7. BANANA AND CHOCOLATE PORRIDGE

Prep + Cook time: 25 min | **Serving:** 2 People

Ingredients:

» 1 cup oatmeal
» 2 cups of milk
» 1 ripe banana, mashed
» 1 tablespoon of cocoa powder

» 1 pinch of salt
» 1/4 teaspoon cinnamon powder
» 1 tablespoon maple syrup

Preparation:

1. Turn on the air oven to 180°C (350°F) and wait until it reaches temperature.
2. In a saucepan, combine the oatmeal, milk, mashed banana, cocoa powder, salt and cinnamon.
3. Mix the ingredients well and bring everything to a boil over medium heat.
4. Pour the mixture into an air ovenproof dish.
5. Bake the porridge for about 15-20 minutes, or until thick and creamy.
6. Serve the oatmeal hot with a spoonful of maple syrup and, if desired, with a few pieces of banana and chocolate on top.

Nutrition per portion: Calories: 300 kcal- Protein: 10 g- Fat: 7 g- Carbohydrates: 51 g- Fiber: 7 g- Sugars: 17 g

Mash the Banana Thoroughly: To ensure a smooth and consistent texture, mash the banana thoroughly before adding it to the oatmeal mixture. This will help the banana blend seamlessly with the other ingredients, adding natural sweetness and flavor to the porridge.

Stir Regularly While Cooking: While bringing the oatmeal mixture to a boil, make sure to stir it regularly to prevent the oatmeal from sticking to the bottom of the saucepan and to ensure even cooking. This will result in a creamy and well-mixed porridge.

Customize Your Toppings: While the recipe suggests topping the porridge with maple syrup, banana slices, and chocolate pieces, feel free to add other toppings like nuts, seeds, or berries to enhance the flavor and texture. This allows you to tailor the porridge to your personal taste and nutritional preferences.

By following these tips, you'll create a delicious and creamy Banana and Chocolate Porridge that's perfect for a comforting breakfast.

8. FRENCH TOAST

Prep + Cook time: 25 min | **Serving:** 2 People

Ingredients:

» 2 slices of toast
» 2 eggs
» 1/2 cup milk
» 1 tablespoon sugar

» 1/4 teaspoon cinnamon powder
» 1 tablespoon butter
» Maple syrup for serving

Preparation:

1. Turn on the air oven to 180°C (350°F) and wait until it reaches temperature.
2. In a bowl, beat the eggs with the milk, sugar, and cinnamon.
3. Dip the bread slices into the egg-milk mixture until they are completely covered.
4. In a nonstick skillet, melt the butter and brown the French bread slices on both sides.
5. Transfer the bread slices to a baking sheet and bake them in an air oven for about 5 to 7 minutes or until puffy and golden brown.
6. Serve the toast warm with a generous portion of maple syrup.

Nutrition per portion: Calories: 298 kcal kcal- Protein: 11 g- Fat: 13 g- Carbohydrates: 36 g- Fiber: 1 g- Sugars: 23 g

Use thicker bread: To achieve a fluffier and more flavorful French Toast, try using thicker slices of bread, such as brioche or challah. These types of bread absorb the egg and milk mixture better without becoming too soggy, resulting in a tastier and richer final product.

Add a touch of vanilla: Adding a splash of vanilla extract to the egg and milk mixture can significantly enhance the flavor of the French Toast. About 1/2 teaspoon of vanilla extract will give a sweet and inviting aroma.

Infuse flavors into the milk mixture: Heat the milk with a cinnamon stick, a split vanilla bean, or a lemon peel before mixing it with the eggs. This step will infuse the milk with extra flavors, making the French Toast even more aromatic and delicious. Just make sure to cool the milk before adding it to the eggs to avoid cooking the eggs prematurely.

These simple adjustments can make a big difference in the final result of your French Toast!

9. OMELET WITH SPINACH AND CHEESE

Prep + Cook time: 15 min | **Serving:** 2 People

Ingredients:

» 4 eggs
» 1 cup fresh spinach washed and chopped
» 1/4 cup grated cheese (such as parmesan or pecorino)

» 1/2 teaspoon salt
» 1/4 teaspoon black pepper
» 1 tablespoon olive oil

Preparation:

1. Turn on the air oven to 180°C (350°F) and wait until it reaches temperature.
2. In a bowl, beat the eggs with the salt and black pepper.
3. Add the chopped spinach to the egg mixture and mix well.
4. Pour the olive oil into a nonstick skillet about 8 inches in diameter and heat over medium-high heat.
5. Pour the egg and spinach mixture into the pan and distribute evenly.
6. Sprinkle the grated cheese over the omelet.
7. Close the lid of the air oven and bake the frittata for about 12 to 15 minutes or until golden brown and puffy.
8. Remove the frittata from the pan and serve hot.

Nutrition per portion: Calories: 257 kcal- Protein: 17 g- Fat: 20 g- Carbohydrates: 2 g- Fiber: 1 g- Sugars: 1 g

Pre-Cook the Spinach: To avoid excess moisture in your omelet, consider sautéing the spinach for a minute or two before adding it to the egg mixture. This will help reduce water content and ensure a firmer, more cohesive omelet.

Use Freshly Grated Cheese: Freshly-grated cheese melts better and has a richer flavor compared to pre-grated cheese. Grate your cheese just before adding it to the omelet for the best texture and taste.

Don[]t Overbeat the Eggs: When beating the eggs, mix them just until the yolks and whites are combined. Overbeating can incorporate too much air, leading to a tougher texture rather than the desired light and fluffy consistency.

By following these tips, you'll enhance the flavor and texture of your Spinach and Cheese Omelet, creating a delightful and satisfying dish.

10. BANANA AND OATMEAL CHEESE PANCAKES

Prep + Cook time: 12 min | **Serving:** 2 People

Ingredients:

» 2 ripe bananas, mashed
» 1/2 cup oatmeal
» 1 egg
» 1 teaspoon cinnamon powder

» 1 pinch of salt
» Butter or spray oil for air fryer
» Fresh fruit or maple syrup for serving (optional)

Preparation:

1. In a bowl, mix mashed bananas with oatmeal, egg, cinnamon, and salt until smooth.
2. Form balls with the mixture and crush them lightly to form pancakes.
3. Grease the basket of the air fryer with a little butter or spray oil to prevent the pancakes from sticking.
4. Place the pancakes in the basket of the air fryer and cook for 6 to 8 minutes or until golden brown and crispy.
5. Flip the pancakes halfway through cooking to ensure even cooking on both sides.
6. Once cooked, serve the pancakes warm with fresh fruit or maple syrup, if desired.

Nutrition per portion: Calories: 230 kcal- Protein: 7 g- Fat: 6 g- Carbohydrates: 43 g- Fiber: 6 g- Sugars: 17 g

Use Ripe Bananas: The riper the bananas, the sweeter and more flavorful your pancakes will be. Ripe bananas also mash more easily and incorporate better into the batter, resulting in a smoother mixture.

Preheat the Air Fryer: Ensure the air fryer is preheated to the correct temperature before adding the pancakes. This helps them cook evenly and achieve a nice, crispy texture.

Avoid Overcrowding: Place the pancakes in the air fryer basket with enough space between them to allow for proper air circulation. This ensures that the pancakes cook evenly and become golden brown on all sides.

By following these tips, you'll enhance the flavor, texture, and overall quality of your Banana and Oatmeal Cheese Pancakes.

APERITIF SNACK RECIPES

11. BRUSCHETTE WITH SUN-DRIED TOMATOES AND MOZZARELLA CHEESE

Prep + Cook time: 10 min | **Serving:** 4 People

Ingredients:

» 4 slices of rustic bread
» 4 sun-dried tomatoes
» 1/2 cup fresh mozzarella cheese, cut into cubes

» 1 clove of garlic, peeled and cut in half
» 2 tablespoons olive oil
» Salt and black pepper to taste

Preparation:

1. Turn on the oven to 200°C and wait until it reaches temperature.
2. Dice the sun-dried tomatoes and place them in a bowl with the fresh mozzarella. Add a pinch of salt and black pepper and mix well.
3. bread slices and drizzle with the olive oil.
4. Spread the sun-dried tomato and mozzarella mixture evenly over the bread.
5. Place the bruschetta in the air fryer and cook for 6 to 8 minutes or until the bread is golden brown and crispy.
6. Serve the bruschetta hot.

Nutrition per portion: Calories: 194.5 kcal-Proteins: 5.5 g- Fats: 11 g- Carbohydrates:20 g- Fibers: 2 g- Sugars: 5 g

Choose Quality Ingredients: Opt for high-quality rustic bread, flavorful sun-dried tomatoes, and fresh mozzarella cheese. The better the quality of your ingredients, the tastier your bruschetta will be.

Prep the Bread Properly: Before adding the toppings, lightly toast the bread slices. Rubbing the toasted bread with a cut garlic clove adds a subtle garlic flavor that enhances the overall taste of the bruschetta.

Evenly Distribute the Toppings: Make sure to evenly spread the sun-dried tomato and mozzarella mixture over the toasted bread slices. This ensures that every bite is bursting with flavor and toppings.

Following these tips will help you create flavorful and perfectly crispy Bruschette with Sun-Dried Tomatoes and Mozzarella Cheese.

12. OLIVE ALL'ASCOLANA

Prep + Cook time: 15 min | **Serving:** 4 People

Ingredients:

» 20 pitted green olives
» 1/2 cup breadcrumbs
» 1/4 cup grated cheese (e.g., parmesan or pecorino)
» 1 egg, beaten

» 1/2 teaspoon salt
» 1/4 teaspoon black pepper
» 1/4 teaspoon nutmeg
» 1 tablespoon chopped fresh parsley
» Olive oil to taste

Preparation:

1. Turn on the oven to 200°C and wait until it reaches temperature.
2. In a bowl, mix the breadcrumbs, grated cheese, salt, black pepper, nutmeg, and chopped parsley.
3. Fill each olive with some of the breadcrumb and cheese mixture, pressing lightly to make the filling stick.
4. Dip the olives in the beaten egg yolk and then dip them in the remaining breadcrumbs, making the breadcrumbs adhere well.
5. Spread the breaded olives in the air fryer and drizzle with a little olive oil.
6. Cook the olives for 10 to 12 minutes, or until they are golden and crispy on the outside and warm on the inside.
7. Serve the olives all'ascolana hot.

Nutrition per portion: Calories: 129.5 kcal - Protein: 5 g- Fat: 10 g- Carbohydrates: 12 g- Fiber: 1 g- Sugars: 1 g

Select firm olives: Opt for firm green olives for stuffing, as they hold their shape better during cooking and provide a satisfying texture contrast to the crispy breadcrumb coating. Soft olives might become mushy during the cooking process.

Enhance the filling: Experiment with adding additional ingredients to the breadcrumb and cheese mixture for a flavor boost. Consider incorporating finely chopped garlic, lemon zest, or a pinch of chili flakes to add complexity to the filling.

Ensure proper breading: To ensure the breadcrumb coating adheres well and forms a crispy crust, pat the olives dry before dipping them in the beaten egg and breadcrumbs. Excess moisture can prevent the breadcrumbs from sticking properly, resulting in a less crispy texture.

13. CROSTINI WITH LIVER PATE

Prep + Cook time: 15 min | **Serving:** 4 People

Ingredients:

- » 4 slices of homemade bread
- » 100 g liver pate
- » 2 tablespoons butter
- » 1/2 cup dry white wine
- » Salt and black pepper to taste
- » Chopped fresh parsley for decoration

Preparation:

1. Turn on the oven to 180°C (350°F) and wait until it reaches temperature.
2. In a frying pan, melt the butter over medium heat. Add the liver pate and stir well until the pate has melted and blended with the butter.
3. Add the white wine and continue stirring for a few minutes until the liquid has evaporated.
4. Toast the bread slices in the air fryer for 2-3 minutes, or until crisp and golden brown.
5. Spread the liver pate over the toasted bread slices.
6. Close the lid of the air fryer and cook the croutons for another 6-8 minutes, or until they are hot and crispy on the outside.
7. Decorate the croutons with fresh chopped parsley and serve hot.

Nutrition per portion: Calories: 241.25 kcal- Protein: 7 g- Fat: 14 g- Carbohydrates: 13 g- Fiber: 1 g- Sugars: 1 g

Choose high-quality liver pate: Opt for a high-quality liver pate to ensure a rich flavor and smooth texture. Consider making your pate or selecting one from a reputable source for the best taste experience.

Infuse extra flavor: Enhance the flavor of the liver pate by incorporating aromatic ingredients such as minced garlic, finely chopped shallots, or a splash of brandy or cognac. Sauté these additions with the butter before adding the liver pate to deepen the flavor profile.

Experiment with bread varieties: While homemade bread is delicious, consider experimenting with different bread varieties to complement the liver pate. Try using crusty baguette slices, whole grain bread, or even rye bread for added texture and flavor complexity.

By following these tips, you can create Crostini with Liver Pate that is bursting with flavor and perfect for any occasion!

14. PINZIMONIO WITH FRESH VEGETABLES AND YOGURT SAUCE

Prep + Cook time: 15 min | **Serving:** 4 People

Ingredients:

» 1 carrot, cut into sticks
» 1 celery, cut into sticks
» 1 bell bell pepper, cut into sticks
» 1 cucumber, cut into sticks

» 1 cup Greek yogurt
» 2 tablespoons lemon juice
» Salt and black pepper to taste

Preparation:

1. Wash and cut the vegetables into sticks.
2. In a bowl, mix Greek yogurt, lemon juice, salt, and black pepper until smooth.
3. Arrange the vegetables on a serving plate and serve with the yogurt sauce.

Nutrition per portion: Calories: 60 kcal- Protein: 4 g- Fat: 1 g- Carbohydrates: 9 g- Fiber: 2 g- Sugars: 5 g

Add herbs for freshness: Incorporate chopped fresh herbs, such as basil, parsley, or dill, into the yogurt sauce for added freshness and flavor. Herbs can elevate the overall taste of the sauce and complement the vegetables beautifully.

Include garlic for depth: For a flavor boost, mince a clove of garlic and mix it into the yogurt sauce. Garlic adds depth and complexity to the sauce, enhancing its overall taste. Adjust the amount according to your preference for garlic intensity.

Sprinkle with toasted nuts or seeds: Before serving, sprinkle the vegetable platter with toasted nuts or seeds, such as pine nuts, almonds, or sesame seeds. Toasted nuts or seeds add a satisfying crunch and nuttiness to the dish, elevating its texture and flavor profile.

By incorporating these tips, you can create a Pinzimonio with Fresh Vegetables and Yogurt Sauce that is not only delicious but also visually appealing and nutritious!

Motivation: We have decided to include this recipe in our Breville air fryer cookbook because, although it does not require cooking, it is an ideal accompaniment to many main dishes prepared with the air fryer. Pinzimonio with Fresh Vegetables and Yogurt Sauce is not only delicious and visually appealing but also extremely healthy. It is perfect for balancing meals and adding a fresh and nutritious component to your daily diet. Additionally, its quick and simple preparation makes it an excellent choice to enhance any menu.

15. TUNA AND POTATO MEATBALLS

Prep + Cook time: 20 min | **Serving:** 4 People

Ingredients:

- » 1 can of canned tuna, drained
- » 2 medium potatoes, boiled and mashed
- » 1 egg, beaten
- » 1/2 cup breadcrumbs
- » 1/4 cup grated cheese (e.g., parmesan or pecorino)
- » 1 clove of garlic, minced
- » 1 tablespoon fresh parsley, chopped
- » 1/2 teaspoon salt
- » 1/4 teaspoon black pepper
- » Olive oil to taste

Preparation:

1. Turn on the air fryer to 200°C and wait until it reaches temperature.
2. In a bowl, mix drained tuna, mashed potatoes, beaten egg, breadcrumbs, grated cheese, minced garlic, chopped fresh parsley, salt, and black pepper until smooth.
3. Take a small amount of the mixture and form patties the size of a walnut.
4. Spread the patties in the air fryer and drizzle with a little olive oil.
5. Cook the meatballs for 10-12 minutes, or until they are golden and crispy on the outside and hot on the inside.
6. Serve the tuna and potato meatballs hot.

Nutrition per portion: Calories: 190 kcal- Protein: 12 g- Fat: 7 g- Carbohydrates: 20 g- Fibers: 2 g- Sugars: 1 g

Enhance with herbs and spices: Add extra flavor to your meatball mixture by incorporating additional herbs and spices. Consider adding a pinch of dried oregano, thyme, or paprika for added depth of flavor. You can also experiment with fresh herbs like basil or cilantro for a burst of freshness.

Incorporate onions for sweetness: Sauté finely chopped onions until they're soft and translucent, then let them cool before adding them to the meatball mixture. Onions add a subtle sweetness and moisture to the meatballs, enhancing their overall taste and texture.

Serve with dipping sauce: Prepare a tangy dipping sauce to accompany your tuna and potato meatballs. Mix Greek yogurt with a squeeze of lemon juice, a dash of olive oil, and a sprinkle of salt and pepper. Optionally, add chopped fresh herbs like dill or chives for extra flavor. This sauce adds a refreshing contrast to the savory meatballs.

By incorporating these tips, you can elevate the flavor and texture of your Tuna and Potato Meatballs for a delightful meal or appetizer!

16. BAKED POTATO CHIPS

Ingredients:

- » 2 medium potatoes, cut into sticks
- » 2 tablespoons olive oil
- » 1/2 teaspoon salt
- » 1/4 teaspoon black pepper

Preparation:

1. Turn on the air fryer to 200°C and wait until it reaches temperature.
2. In a bowl, mix the potato sticks, olive oil, salt, and black pepper until all the potatoes are well coated.
3. Spread the chips in the air fryer and cook for 20-25 minutes or until crisp and golden brown.
4. Remove the fries from the air fryer and serve piping hot.

Nutrition per portion: Calories: 140 kcal- Protein: 2 g- Fat: 7 g- Carbohydrates: 12 g- Fiber: 2 g- Sugars: 1 g

Slice the potatoes evenly: For consistent cooking, aim to cut the potato sticks into uniform thickness. This ensures that all the chips cook at the same rate, resulting in a batch of evenly crispy chips.

Soak the potato sticks: Soaking the sliced potatoes in cold water for about 30 minutes before cooking can help remove excess starch, resulting in crispier chips. After soaking, pat the potato sticks dry thoroughly with paper towels to remove any excess moisture before seasoning and cooking.

Season generously: Don't be shy with the seasoning! While the recipe calls for salt and black pepper, feel free to experiment with different seasonings to add extra flavor. Try sprinkling the potato sticks with garlic powder, paprika, or grated Parmesan cheese before cooking for a tasty twist on classic potato chips.

By following these tips, you can achieve crispy, flavorful Baked Potato Chips that are sure to be a hit with your family and friends!

17. ARANCINI WITH MEAT SAUCE

Prep + Cook time: 30 min | **Serving:** 4 People

Ingredients:

» 1 cup Arborio rice
» 1/2 cup meat sauce
» 1/4 cup grated cheese (e.g., parmesan or pecorino)

» 1 egg, beaten
» 1/2 cup breadcrumbs
» Olive oil to taste

Preparation:

1. Turn on the air fryer to 200°C and wait until it reaches temperature.
2. Prepare the Arborio rice according to the instructions on the package and let it cool.
3. In a bowl, mix the cooled rice, meat sauce, grated cheese, and beaten egg until smooth.
4. Take a small amount of the mixture and form walnut-sized balls.
5. Dip the balls in breadcrumbs, making the breadcrumbs stick well.
6. Spread the arancini in the air fryer and drizzle with a little olive oil.
7. Cook the arancini for 10 to 12 minutes, or until golden and crispy on the outside and hot on the inside.
8. Serve the arancini with meat sauce hot.

Nutrition per portion: Calories: 190 kcal- Protein: 9 g- Fat: 6 g- Carbohydrates: 20 g- Fiber: 2 g- Sugars: 2 g

Use cold rice: For the best texture, use cold, leftover Arborio rice for making arancini. Cold rice holds its shape better and is easier to work with when forming the balls. If you're using freshly cooked rice, spread it out on a baking sheet and let it cool completely before using it to make arancini.

Add flavor to the rice: Enhance the flavor of the rice mixture by seasoning it with herbs and spices. Consider adding a pinch of dried oregano, basil, or thyme to the rice mixture for an extra layer of flavor. You can also mix in finely chopped parsley or grated lemon zest for a fresh and zesty twist.

Try different fillings: While meat sauce is a classic filling for arancini, don't be afraid to get creative with your fillings. Experiment with different ingredients like mozzarella cheese, peas, diced ham, or sautéed mushrooms for a variety of flavors and textures. Just make sure to fully encase the filling in the rice mixture to prevent it from leaking out during cooking.

By incorporating these tips, you can create Arancini with Meat Sauce that are bursting with flavor and perfect for any occasion!

18. MINI QUICHE WITH SPINACH AND CHEESE

Prep + Cook time: 20 min + 15-18 min | **Serving:** 4 People

Ingredients:

» 1 roll of puff pastry
» 1 cup fresh spinach, chopped
» 1/2 cup grated cheese (such as parmesan or pecorino)

» 2 eggs
» 1/2 cup milk
» Salt and pepper to taste

Preparation:

1. Turn on the oven to 180°C (350°F).
2. Unroll the puff pastry and cut it into squares of the desired size.
3. Lay the puff pastry squares in a muffin tin, making the pastry stick well to the walls of the tin.
4. In a bowl, mix chopped spinach, grated cheese,

eggs, milk, salt, and pepper until smooth.
5. Pour the spinach and cheese mixture into the puff pastry shells, filling them about 2/3 full.
6. Bake the mini quiches for 15 to 18 minutes or until puffy and golden brown on top.
7. Remove the mini quiches from the oven and serve warm.

Nutrition per portion: Calories: 450 kcal- Protein: 14 g- Fat: 16 g- Carbohydrates: 26 g- Fiber: 0 g- Sugars: 11,5 g

Pre-cook the spinach: To prevent excess moisture in your quiches, consider sautéing the chopped spinach in a skillet for a few minutes until wilted before adding it to the quiche mixture. This will help concentrate the flavor of the spinach and prevent the quiches from becoming watery during baking.

Add flavor with seasonings: Experiment with different seasonings to enhance the flavor of your quiches. Consider adding a pinch of nutmeg or a dash of garlic powder to the spinach and cheese mixture for added depth of flavor. You can also try incorporating fresh herbs like thyme or basil for a burst of freshness.

Customize with additional ingredients: While spinach and cheese make a classic combination, feel free to customize your mini quiches with additional ingredients to suit your taste. Try adding diced cooked bacon, caramelized onions, sliced mushrooms, or chopped sun-dried tomatoes for extra flavor and texture. Just be mindful not to overfill the pastry shells to ensure they bake evenly.

By following these tips, you can create Mini Quiche with Spinach and Cheese that are flavorful, perfectly cooked, and sure to impress!

FISH AND SEAFOOD RECIPES

19. SHRIMP AND PINEAPPLE SKEWERS

Prep + Cook time: 15 min | **Serving:** 2 People

Ingredients:

- » 8 large shrimp, shelled and cleaned
- » 8 cubes of fresh pineapple
- » 1 tablespoon olive oil
- » 1 clove of garlic, minced
- » 1 teaspoon sweet paprika
- » Salt and black pepper to taste

Preparation:

1. Turn on the air fryer to 180°C (350°F) and wait until it reaches the temperature.
2. In a bowl, mix olive oil with minced garlic, sweet paprika, salt, and black pepper.
3. Add the shrimp to the seasoning mixture and mix well to coat them evenly.
4. Take a pineapple cube and thread it through a kebab skewer, then thread a shrimp through it.
5. Continue alternating the pineapples and shrimp on the skewers until all ingredients are used up.
6. Place the skewers in the basket of the air fryer and cook for about 5 to 7 minutes, or until the shrimp are cooked and the pineapple is lightly browned.
7. Turn the skewers halfway through cooking to ensure even cooking on both sides.
8. Once cooked, serve the shrimp and pineapple skewers warm and garnish with fresh herbs, such as mint or parsley, if desired.

Nutrition per portion: Calories: 144 kcal- Protein: 10 g- Fats: 8 g- Carbohydrates: 9 g- Fibers: 1 g- Sugars: 5 g

Marinate for extra flavor: For an extra burst of flavor, marinate the shrimp in the seasoning mixture for about 15-30 minutes before threading them onto the skewers. This allows the flavors to penetrate the shrimp and pineapple cubes, resulting in a more flavorful dish.

Use wooden skewers: If you're using wooden skewers, make sure to soak them in water for about 30 minutes before threading the shrimp and pineapple onto them. This helps prevent the skewers from burning in the air fryer and ensures they cook evenly.

Add a citrusy kick: Enhance the flavor of your skewers by adding a squeeze of fresh lime or lemon juice to the seasoning mixture. The citrusy acidity pairs wonderfully with the sweetness of the pineapple and the savory flavors of the shrimp, adding brightness to the dish.

20. POTATO AND CHEESE CROQUETTES

Prep + Cook time: 30 min | **Serving:** 2 People

Ingredients:

» 2 large potatoes
» 1/2 cup grated cheese (cheddar, parmesan, pecorino, to taste)
» 1 egg
» 1/4 cup breadcrumbs
» 2 tablespoons extra virgin olive oil
» Salt and black pepper to taste

Preparation:

1. Preheat the Breville Smart Pro air fryer to 200°C.
2. Peel the potatoes and cut them into cubes. Steam the potatoes or cook them in boiling water until soft but not flaky.
3. Mash the potatoes with a fork or masher until smooth.
4. Add the grated cheese, egg, bread crumbs, olive oil, salt, and black pepper to the mashed potatoes. Mix well until smooth.
5. Form croquettes with the potato and cheese mixture, being careful not to make them too large.
6. Place the croquettes in the basket of the Breville Smart Pro air fryer and cook for about 10 to 12 minutes or until golden brown and crispy.
7. Turn the croquettes halfway through cooking to ensure even cooking on both sides.
8. Once cooked, serve the potato and cheese croquettes warm and garnish with fresh herbs, such as parsley or mint, if desired.

Nutrition per portion: Calories: 456 kcal- Protein: 18 g- Fat: 24 g- Carbohydrates: 44 g- Fiber: 4 g- Sugars: 2 g

Choose the right potato: Opt for starchy potatoes like Russet or Yukon Gold, as they yield a fluffier texture when mashed. Avoid using waxy potatoes, as they can result in a dense and gluey consistency.

Enhance with herbs and spices: Add extra flavor to your croquettes by incorporating herbs and spices into the mixture. Consider adding chopped fresh herbs like chives, parsley, or thyme for a burst of freshness. You can also add a pinch of garlic powder, smoked paprika, or cayenne pepper for additional depth of flavor.

21. PINEAPPLE COD FILLETS

Prep + Cook time: 25 min | **Serving:** 2 People

Ingredients:

- » 2 cod fillets
- » 1/2 cup flour
- » 1/2 cup breadcrumbs
- » 1 egg
- » 1 tablespoon sweet paprika
- » Salt and black pepper to taste
- » Spray oil for air fryer

Preparation:

1. Preheat the Breville Smart Pro air fryer to 200°C.
2. In a bowl, mix the flour with the sweet paprika, salt, and pepper.
3. In another bowl, beat the egg with a fork.
4. In a third bowl, place the breadcrumbs.
5. Dip the cod fillets in the flour, then in the egg, and finally in the breadcrumbs.
6. Place the cod fillets in the basket of the Breville Smart Pro air fryer and spray with a little spray oil.
7. Cook for about 10-12 minutes, or until golden brown and crispy.
8. Turn the cod fillets halfway through cooking to ensure even cooking on both sides.
9. Once cooked, serve the cod fillets hot with a squeeze of fresh lemon juice and garnish with fresh herbs, such as parsley or mint, if desired.

Nutrition per portion: Calories: 355 kcal- Protein: 32 g- Fat: 4 g- Carbohydrates: 42 g- Fiber: 2 g- Sugars: 1 g

Add pineapple for a tropical twist: For an extra burst of flavor and juiciness, consider incorporating pineapple into the recipe. You can either coat the cod fillets with pineapple juice before breading them or serve the cooked fillets with a side of pineapple salsa or chunks for a tropical twist.

Enhance the breading: Elevate the flavor of the breading by incorporating additional herbs and spices. Consider adding dried herbs like thyme, oregano, or basil to the breadcrumbs, along with a pinch of garlic powder or onion powder for extra flavor depth. This will add complexity to the dish and complement the mild flavor of the cod.

22. PINEAPPLE SQUID

Prep + Cook time: 15 min | **Serving:** 2 People

Ingredients:

» 250 g squid rings
» 1/2 cup cornmeal
» 1 teaspoon sweet paprika
» Salt and black pepper to taste
» Spray oil for air fryer

Preparation:

1. Preheat the Breville Smart Pro air fryer to 200°C.
2. In a bowl, mix cornmeal with sweet paprika, salt, and pepper.
3. Dip the squid rings in the cornmeal mixture, being careful to shake off any excess flour.
4. Place the squid rings in the basket of the Breville Smart Pro air fryer and spray with a little spray oil.
5. Cook for about 8 to 10 minutes, or until golden brown and crispy.
6. Turn the squid rings halfway through cooking to ensure even cooking on both sides.
7. Once cooked, serve the squid rings hot with a spicy tomato sauce or lemon mayonnaise, if desired.

Nutrition per portion: Calories: 190 kcal- Protein: 18 g- Fat: 3 g- Carbohydrates: 24 g- Fiber: 2 g- Sugars: 1 g

Tenderize the squid: Before breading the squid rings, consider tenderizing them to ensure they are not tough or chewy after cooking. You can tenderize the squid by soaking it in milk for about 30 minutes before breading. The enzymes in the milk help break down the proteins in the squid, resulting in a more tender texture.

Add extra flavor to the coating: Enhance the flavor of the cornmeal coating by adding additional spices or herbs. Consider mixing in garlic powder, onion powder, or dried herbs like thyme or oregano to the cornmeal mixture. This will infuse the squid with extra flavor and complement its natural sweetness.

Serve with dipping sauce: **Prep**are a flavorful dipping sauce to accompany the Pineapple Squid for added taste and variety. A spicy tomato sauce or lemon mayonnaise would pair well with the crispy squid rings. Alternatively, you can serve them with a classic tartar sauce or aioli for a creamy and tangy contrast.

By following these tips, you can create a Pineapple Squid that is crispy, flavorful, and sure to be a hit with your family and friends!

23. PINEAPPLE COCONUT SHRIMP

Prep + Cook time: 15 min | **Serving:** 2 People

Ingredients:

» 250 g shelled and cleaned shrimp
» 1/2 cup coconut flour
» 1 egg

» 1/2 cup breadcrumbs
» Salt and black pepper to taste
» Spray oil for air fryer

Preparation:

1. Preheat the air fryer to 200°C.
2. In a bowl, beat the egg with a fork.
3. In another bowl, mix coconut flour with breadcrumbs, salt, and pepper.
4. Dip the shrimp into the beaten egg, then coat them with the mixture of coconut flour and breadcrumbs.
5. Place the shrimp in the basket of the Breville Smart Pro air fryer and spray with a little oil spray.
6. Cook for about 8 to 10 minutes, or until golden brown and crispy.
7. Turn the shrimp halfway through cooking to ensure even cooking on both sides.
8. Once cooked, serve the coconut shrimp hot with a sweet and sour sauce or spicy mango salsa, if desired.

Nutrition per portion: Calories: 380 kcal- Protein: 23 g- Fat: 16 g- Carbohydrates: 34 g- Fiber: 9 g- Sugars: 4 g

Prep the shrimp properly: Before breading the shrimp, ensure they are properly shelled, cleaned, and patted dry with paper towels. Excess moisture on the shrimp can prevent the breading from sticking properly and result in a less crispy coating.

Enhance the coconut flavor: For an extra burst of coconut flavor, consider incorporating shredded coconut into the breading mixture along with the coconut flour and breadcrumbs. This will add texture and amplify the coconut flavor in every bite.

Serve with complementary sauce: Pair the crispy coconut shrimp with a flavorful dipping sauce that complements the tropical flavors. A sweet and tangy sauce like sweet chili sauce or a creamy coconut curry dip would be perfect. Alternatively, a mango salsa with jalapeños for a hint of heat can add a refreshing contrast to the crispy shrimp.

By following these tips, you can create Pineapple Coconut Shrimp that are crispy, flavorful, and perfect for a delicious and satisfying meal!

24. PINEAPPLE TUNA MEATBALLS

Prep + Cook time: 15 min | **Serving:** 2 People

Ingredients:

- 1 can of tuna in oil (100 g)
- 1 egg
- 1/2 cup breadcrumbs
- 1/4 cup grated cheese (parmesan, apiacere)
- 1 tablespoon of mayonnaise
- 1 teaspoon of mustard
- Salt and black pepper to taste
- Spray oil for air fryer

Preparation:

1. Preheat the Breville Smart Pro air fryer to 200°C.
2. In a bowl, drain the tuna from the oil and crumble it with a fork.
3. Add inside the bowl the breadcrumbs, egg, grated cheese, mayonnaise, mustard, salt, and pepper. Mix well until the mixture is smooth.
4. Form patties with the tuna mixture, being careful not to make them too large.
5. Place the patties in the basket of the Breville Smart Pro air fryer and spray with a little spray oil.
6. Cook for about 10 to 12 minutes, or until golden brown and crispy.
7. Turn the patties halfway through cooking to ensure even cooking on both sides.
8. Once cooked, serve the tuna meatballs warm with a yogurt and dill sauce, if desired.

Nutrition per portion: Calories: 320 kcal-Protein: 20 g- Fat: 12 g- Carbohydrates: 22 g- Fiber: 1 g- Sugars: 2 g

Enhance with pineapple: Add a tropical twist to your tuna meatballs by incorporating diced pineapple into the mixture. The sweetness of the pineapple will complement the savory tuna and add a burst of flavor. Make sure to drain the pineapple well to avoid excess moisture in the meatball mixture.

Serve with tangy sauce: Pair the tuna meatballs with a tangy sauce to balance out the flavors. **Prep**are a yogurt and dill sauce by mixing Greek yogurt with chopped fresh dill, lemon juice, salt, and pepper. Alternatively, you can serve the meatballs with a zesty tzatziki sauce or a spicy sriracha mayo for added kick.

By incorporating these tips, you can create Pineapple Tuna Meatballs that are flavorful, moist, and perfect for a quick and satisfying meal!

25. PINEAPPLE CHICKEN WINGS

Prep + Cook time: 25 min | **Serving:** 2 People

Ingredients:

» 6 chicken wings
» 1/2 cup flour
» 1 teaspoon sweet paprika

» 1 teaspoon garlic powder
» Salt and black pepper to taste
» Spray oil for air fryer

Preparation:

1. Preheat the Breville Smart Pro air fryer to 200°C.
2. In a bowl, mix the flour with the sweet paprika, garlic powder, salt, and pepper.
3. Dip chicken wings in flour mixture, being careful to shake off excess flour.
4. Place the chicken wings in the basket of the Breville Smart Pro air fryer and spray with a little oil spray.
5. Cook for about 18 to 20 minutes, or until golden brown and crispy.
6. Turn the chicken wings halfway through cooking to ensure even cooking on both sides.
7. Once cooked, serve the chicken wings hot with a barbecue sauce or honey-mustard sauce, if desired.

Nutrition per portion: Calories: 260 kcal- Protein: 18 g- Fat: 10 g- Carbohydrates: 33 g- Fiber: 1 g- Sugars: 1

Marinate for extra flavor: Before coating the chicken wings with flour, consider marinating them in a pineapple-based marinade for added flavor. Pineapple juice, soy sauce, garlic, ginger, and a touch of brown sugar can create a delicious marinade. Let the chicken wings soak in the marinade for at least 30 minutes (or overnight for maximum flavor) before breading and air frying. This will infuse the wings with a tropical sweetness and enhance their overall taste.

Add a crunchy coating: For an extra crispy texture, try adding crushed pineapple-flavored cornflakes or panko breadcrumbs to the flour mixture. The added crunchiness will complement the tender chicken meat inside. You can also mix in some shredded coconut for a tropical twist. Ensure the chicken wings are evenly coated with the crunchy coating before air frying to achieve a crispy exterior.

Glaze with pineapple sauce: Instead of serving the chicken wings with barbecue or honey-mustard sauce, consider making a homemade pineapple glaze. Combine pineapple juice, soy sauce, honey, minced garlic, and ginger in a saucepan.

26. SEA BASS IN PINEAPPLE AIR FRYER

Prep + Cook time: 20 min | **Serving:** 2 People

Ingredients:

- 2 sea bass fillets
- 1/2 cup breadcrumbs
- 1/4 cup grated cheese (cheddar, parmesan to taste)
- 1 clove of garlic, minced
- 1 tablespoon chopped parsley
- Salt and black pepper to taste
- Spray oil for air fryer

Preparation:

1. Preheat the Breville Smart Pro air fryer to 200°C.
2. In a bowl, mix the breadcrumbs with the grated cheese, minced garlic, parsley, salt and pepper.
3. Toss the sea bass fillets in the breadcrumb mixture, making sure to cover them well.
4. Place the sea bass fillets in the basket of the Breville Smart Pro air fryer and spray with a little spray oil.
5. Cook for about 12 to 15 minutes, or until golden brown and crispy.
6. Turn the sea bass fillets halfway through cooking to ensure even cooking on both sides.
7. Once cooked, serve the sea bass fillets hot with a lemon sauce and fresh herbs, such as thyme or rosemary

Nutrition per portion: Calories: 183 kcal - Protein: 25 g - Fat: 7 g - Carbohydrates: 12 g - Fiber: 0.5g - Sugars: 0.5 g

Incorporate pineapple for a tropical twist: Add diced pineapple to the breadcrumb mixture for an extra burst of sweetness and tropical flavor. The pineapple will complement the savory sea bass and add a refreshing element to the dish. Make sure to drain the pineapple well to avoid excess moisture, which can affect the crispiness of the breadcrumb coating.

Season the breadcrumb mixture: Enhance the flavor of the breadcrumb mixture by seasoning it generously. Consider adding additional herbs and spices such as lemon zest, smoked paprika, or dried herbs like basil and thyme. This will add depth of flavor to the dish and elevate its taste.

Serve with a tangy lemon sauce: Instead of just serving the sea bass with lemon wedges, prepare a tangy lemon sauce to drizzle over the cooked fillets. Combine lemon juice, olive oil, minced garlic, chopped fresh herbs like parsley or dill, salt, and pepper in a small saucepan. Simmer the mixture until it thickens slightly, then drizzle it over the cooked sea bass fillets just before serving. This will add brightness and acidity to the dish, balancing the richness of the sea bass and enhancing its overall flavor.

27. PINEAPPLE SWEET POTATO FRIES

Prep + Cook time: 25 min | **Serving:** 2 People

Ingredients:

» 2 medium sweet potatoes
» 1 teaspoon olive oil

» 1/2 teaspoon salt
» 1/2 teaspoon sweet paprika

Preparation:

1. Preheat the Breville Smart Pro air fryer to 200°C.
2. Peel the sweet potatoes and cut them into thin slices.
3. In a bowl, mix the sweet potato slices with the olive oil, salt and sweet paprika.
4. Place the sweet potato slices in the basket of the Breville Smart Pro air fryer.
5. Cook for about 15 to 20 minutes, or until crisp and lightly browned.
6. Turn the sweet potato slices halfway through cooking to ensure even cooking on both sides.
7. Once cooked, serve the sweet potato fries hot with yogurt and garlic sauce, if desired.

Nutrition per portion: Calories: 140 kcal- Protein: 2 g- Fat: 3 g- Carbohydrates: 22 g- Fiber: 4 g- Sugars: 7 g

Ensure even cutting: For uniform cooking, cut the sweet potatoes into evenly sized slices or sticks. Using a mandoline slicer can help achieve consistent thickness, which is key for ensuring that all the fries cook at the same rate and achieve a crispy texture.

Avoid overcrowding: Arrange the sweet potato slices in a single layer in the air fryer basket without overlapping them. Overcrowding can prevent the fries from getting crispy. If needed, cook the fries in batches to ensure they are all evenly cooked and crispy.

Experiment with additional seasonings: Enhance the flavor profile by adding a pinch of cinnamon or a touch of cayenne pepper to the seasoning mix. This can create a sweet and spicy contrast that pairs well with the natural sweetness of the sweet potatoes. Additionally, tossing the fries with a bit of cornstarch before air frying can help achieve an extra crispy exterior.

By following these tips, you can create perfectly crispy and flavorful Pineapple Sweet Potato Fries that are a delicious and healthy addition to any meal!

28. PINEAPPLE CORN FRITTERS

Prep + Cook time: 15 min | **Serving:** 2 People

Ingredients:

» 1 cup cornmeal
» 1/2 cup 00 flour
» 2 teaspoons baking powder
» 1/2 teaspoon salt

» 1 egg
» 1/2 cup milk
» 1/4 cup melted butter
» Spray oil for air fryer

Preparation:

1. Preheat the Breville Smart Pro air fryer to 200°C.
2. In a bowl, mix cornmeal, 00 flour, baking powder, and salt.
3. In another bowl, beat the egg with the milk and melted butter.
4. Combine the dry ingredients with the liquid mixture and mix well until a smooth dough is obtained.
5. Place the dough in the basket of the Breville Smart Pro air fryer and spray with a little oil spray.
6. Cook for about 8-10 minutes, or until pancakes are golden brown and puffy.
7. Flip the pancakes halfway through cooking to ensure even cooking on both sides.
8. Once cooked, serve the corn pancakes hot with maple syrup or cheese sauces, if desired.

Nutrition per portion: Calories: 623 kcal- Protein: 11 g- Fat: 30 g- Carbohydrates: 73 g- Fiber: 5 g- Sugars: 5 g

Add Pineapple for Extra Flavor: Incorporate finely diced pineapple into the batter to add a sweet, tropical twist to your fritters. Ensure the pineapple pieces are well-drained and lightly patted dry to avoid adding excess moisture, which could affect the texture of the fritters.

Optimal Batter Consistency: Ensure the batter is the right consistency - not too thick or too thin. If the batter is too thick, the fritters might be dense; if too thin, they might spread too much. You can adjust the consistency by adding a little more milk if it's too thick or a bit more flour if it's too thin.

Use Parchment Paper: To prevent sticking and ensure easy flipping, you can place a piece of parchment paper in the air fryer basket before adding the batter. This helps maintain the shape of the fritters and makes cleanup easier. Make sure to lightly spray the parchment paper with oil before adding the batter.

29. PINEAPPLE AIR FRYER FRIED RAVIOLI

Prep + Cook time: 20 min | **Serving:** 2 People

Ingredients:

» 250 g cheese ravioli
» 1 cup of breadcrumbs
» 1/2 cup grated cheese (cheddar, parmesan to taste)
» 1/2 teaspoon garlic powder
» 1/2 teaspoon sweet paprika
» 1 egg
» Salt and black pepper to taste
» Spray oil for air fryer

Preparation:

1. Preheat the Breville Smart Pro air fryer to 200°C.
2. In a bowl, beat the egg with a fork.
3. In another bowl, mix the breadcrumbs with the grated cheese, garlic powder, sweet paprika, salt, and pepper.
4. Dip the ravioli in the egg, then in the breadcrumbs and cheese mixture, making sure to cover them well.
5. Place the ravioli in the basket of the Breville Smart Pro air fryer and spray with a little spray oil.
6. Cook for about 10 to 12 minutes, or until golden brown and crispy.
7. Turn the ravioli halfway through cooking to ensure even cooking on both sides.
8. Once cooked, serve the fried ravioli hot with tomato sauce or cheese sauce, if you sidesider.

Nutrition per portion: - Calories: 500 kcal- Protein: 37 g- Fat: 29 g-Carbohydrates: 72 g- Fiber: 5 g- Sugars: 4 g

Add a Pineapple Twist: Incorporate finely chopped pineapple into the breading mixture for a unique and sweet flavor. Make sure the pineapple is well-drained and patted dry to avoid adding excess moisture. The sweet and tangy pineapple will complement the savory cheese filling beautifully.

Double-Coat for Extra Crispiness: For an extra crispy coating, double-coat the ravioli. After the initial dip in the egg and breadcrumbs mixture, repeat the process by dipping the coated ravioli back into the egg and then into the breadcrumbs mixture again. This will create a thicker, crunchier crust.

Serve with a Complementary Dipping Sauce: Enhance the flavor profile by serving the fried ravioli with a complementary dipping sauce. A pineapple salsa or a sweet chili sauce would pair well with the pineapple-infused breading, adding a refreshing and zesty contrast to the savory ravioli.

30. BANANAS FALAFEL

Prep + Cook time: 20 min | **Serving:** 2 People

Ingredients:

» 1 cup dried chickpeas
» 1/2 onion, chopped
» 3 cloves of garlic, minced
» 1/4 cup chopped fresh parsley
» 1 teaspoon cumin
» 1 teaspoon coriander

» 1/2 teaspoon salt
» 1/4 teaspoon black pepper
» 1/2 cup chopped pineapple
» 1/4 cup chickpea flour
» Spray oil for air fryer

Preparation:

1. Soak dried chickpeas in cold water for about 6 to 8 hours.
2. Rinse and drain the chickpeas well and place them in a food processor along with the onion, garlic, parsley, cumin, coriander, pineapple, salt, and pepper.
3. Grind the ingredients until smooth.
4. Gradually add the chickpea flour to the mixture and mix well.
5. Form balls with dough about the size of 3 cm.
6. Place the balls in the basket of the Breville Smart Pro air fryer and spray with a little oil spray.
7. Cook for about 12 to 15 minutes, or until the falafels are golden brown and crisp, turning them halfway through cooking for even cooking.
8. Serve pineapple falafel hot with a yogurt and garlic sauce, or with hummus and salad to taste.

Nutrition per portion: Calories: 462 kcal - Protein: 22 g - Fat: 6 g - Carbohydrates: 80 g - Fiber: circa 15.75 g - Sugars: circa 13.75 g

Optimize Texture with Proper Chickpea Preparation: Ensure your chickpeas are well-soaked and drained. If they retain too much water, the falafel mixture can become too moist and difficult to form into balls. After soaking, spread the chickpeas out on a clean towel and pat them dry to remove excess moisture.

Balance Flavors with Pineapple: Pineapple adds a unique sweetness to the falafel. Make sure to finely chop the pineapple and drain any excess juice to prevent the mixture from becoming too wet. You can also consider lightly caramelizing the pineapple in a pan before adding it to the mix, which enhances its flavor and reduces moisture.

31. BAKED SALMON WITH LEMON AND HERBS

Prep + Cook time: 20 min | **Serving:** 2 People

Ingredients:

» 2 fresh salmon fillets
» 1 lemon
» 2 tablespoons chopped fresh herbs (parsley, thyme, rosemary, basil)

» 1/4 teaspoon salt
» 1/4 teaspoon black pepper
» Spray oil for air fryer

Preparation:

1. Preheat the oven to 200°C.
2. Cut the lemon into thin slices.
3. In a small bowl, mix the chopped herbs, salt, and black pepper.
4. Place the salmon fillets in the bottom of the basket of the air fryer.
5. Brush or spray the salmon fillets with a little oil spray.
6. Cover the salmon fillets with the lemon slices.
7. Sprinkle chopped herbs over the lemon slices.
8. Cook the salmon for about 10-12 minutes, or until the flesh is soft and flakes easily with a fork.
9. Serve the salmon hot with a squeeze of fresh lemon juice and a garnish of fresh herbs, if desired.

Nutrition per portion: Calories: 190 kcal-Protein: 28 g- Fat: 10 g- Carbohydrates: 4 g- Fiber: 1 g- Sugars: 0.5 g

Ensure Even Cooking with Proper Placement: When placing the salmon fillets in the air fryer, make sure they are in a single layer and not overlapping. This ensures that the hot air circulates evenly around each fillet, promoting even cooking and a consistent texture throughout.

Enhance Flavor with Herb Mixture: To maximize the flavor, gently press the chopped herbs into the lemon slices before placing them on the salmon. This helps the herbs adhere better to the fish and infuses more flavor during cooking. You can also add a little garlic powder or lemon zest to the herb mixture for an extra kick.

Monitor Cooking Time Closely: Salmon can overcook quickly, becoming dry and less flavorful. Start checking the salmon at the 10-minute mark to see if it flakes easily with a fork. The internal temperature should reach about 63°C (145°F). Adjust the cooking time based on the thickness of the fillets and the specific performance of your air fryer.

By following these tips, you'll achieve perfectly cooked, flavorful salmon fillets that are enhanced by the fresh taste of lemon and herbs. Enjoy your dish!

POULTRY RECIPES

32. CHICKEN HUNTING

Prep + Cook time: 30 min | **Serving:** 2 People

Ingredients:

»   2 chicken thighs
»   1 onion
»   1 carrot
»   1 celery stalk
»   1 clove of garlic

»   200 g peeled tomatoes
»   1 glass of dry white wine
»   2 tablespoons of extra virgin olive oil
»   salt and pepper to taste

Preparation:

1. Finely chop the onion, carrot, celery, and garlic and put them in the basket of the air fryer oven.
2. Add the chicken thighs and season with extra virgin olive oil, salt and pepper.
3. Bake at 200°C for about 20-25 minutes, turning the chicken halfway through cooking.
4. Add the peeled tomatoes and dry white wine to the basket of the air fryer oven. Stir well.
5. Cover the air fryer oven basket with a lid or aluminum foil and continue cooking at 200°C for another 10-15 minutes, until the chicken is tender and the sauce has thickened.
6. Serve the chicken cacciatore hot.

Nutrition per portion: Calories: 480 kcal- Protein: 26 g- Fats: 15 g- Carbohydrates: 15 g – Fiber: 2.5g – Sugars: 7.5 g

Use Fresh Herbs for Maximum Flavor: Fresh herbs like parsley, thyme, rosemary, and basil provide the best flavor for this dish. Make sure they are finely chopped to evenly distribute their flavors over the salmon. If fresh herbs are unavailable, dried herbs can be used, but reduce the quantity to about half, as dried herbs are more concentrated.

Ensure Even Cooking with Proper Fillet Placement: Arrange the salmon fillets in a single layer without overlapping in the air fryer basket. This allows hot air to circulate around the fillets, ensuring they cook evenly and develop a nice, crispy exterior.

Monitor Cooking Time for Perfect Doneness: Keep a close eye on the salmon during cooking. The fillets should be cooked until they just start to flake with a fork but are still moist and tender.

33. CHICKEN'S BREAST WITH LEMON

Prep + Cook time: 30 min | **Serving:** 2 People

Ingredients:

- » 2 chicken breasts
- » 1 lemon
- » 1 clove of garlic
- » 2 tablespoons extra virgin olive oil
- » salt and pepper to taste

Preparation:

1. Cut the lemon into thin slices and finely chop the garlic.
2. In a bowl, mix the extra virgin olive oil with the juice of half a lemon, minced garlic, salt and pepper.
3. Brush the chicken breasts with the resulting marinade and lay them in the basket of the air fryer oven.
4. Bake at 200°C for about 20-25 minutes, or until the chicken is golden brown and 100 percent cooked through.
5. Serve the lemon chicken breast hot.

Nutrition per portion: Calories: 282 kcal - Protein: 28 - Fat: 15 g - Carbohydrates: 4 g – Fiber: 1 g – Sugars: 1 g

Marinate for Deeper Flavor: If time permits, let the chicken breasts marinate in the lemon-garlic-olive oil mixture for at least 30 minutes before cooking. This allows the flavors to penetrate the meat, resulting in a more flavorful dish. For even more flavor, you can marinate the chicken in the refrigerator overnight.

Even Cooking and Browning: To ensure even cooking and a nicely browned exterior, make sure the chicken breasts are of similar thickness. If they vary in thickness, use a meat mallet to pound them to an even thickness. This helps in cooking them uniformly and prevents overcooking or undercooking.

Monitor Internal Temperature: Chicken breasts can dry out if overcooked. Use a meat thermometer to check the internal temperature, which should reach 74°C (165°F) for safe consumption. Insert the thermometer into the thickest part of the chicken breast to get an accurate reading.

By following these tips, you can ensure your Chicken Breast with Lemon is flavorful, moist, and perfectly cooked. Enjoy!

34. ROASTED CHICKEN WITH POTATOES

Prep + Cook time: 40 min | **Serving:** 2 People

Ingredients:

» 2 chicken thighs
» 2 potatoes
» 1 onion

» 2 tablespoons extra virgin olive oil
» salt and pepper to taste

Preparation:

1. Cut the potatoes and onion into cubes and place them in a bowl.
2. Combine the chicken thighs and season with extra virgin olive oil, salt and pepper.
3. Transfer everything to the basket of the air fryer oven.
4. Bake at 200°C for about 25-30 minutes, turning the chicken and stirring in the potatoes and onion halfway through cooking.
5. Serve the roast chicken with potatoes hot.

Nutrition per portion: Calories: 420 kcal - Protein: 23 g- Fat: 21 g - Carbohydrates: 35 g – Fiber: 4 g – Sugars: 4.5 g

Preheat the Air Fryer: Ensure the air fryer is preheated to 200°C before adding the chicken and potatoes. This helps achieve a crispy exterior on the chicken and properly roasted potatoes from the start.

Cut Evenly-Sized Pieces: Cut the potatoes and onions into evenly sized cubes to ensure they cook at the same rate. This prevents smaller pieces from burning while waiting for larger ones to cook through. Similarly, if your chicken thighs are of different sizes, consider trimming them to be more uniform or adjusting the cooking time accordingly.

Season Generously and Stir Midway: Season the potatoes, onions, and chicken generously with salt and pepper to enhance their flavors. Stir the vegetables and turn the chicken halfway through cooking to ensure even browning and cooking. This also helps prevent sticking and promotes even heat distribution.

By following these tips, you'll achieve a deliciously roasted chicken with perfectly cooked potatoes and onions, all made conveniently in your air fryer. Enjoy your meal!

35. CHICKEN CURRY

Prep + Cook time: 40 min | **Serving:** 2 People

Ingredients:

- » 2 chicken breasts
- » 1 onion
- » 1 bell bell pepper
- » 1 teaspoon curry powder
- » 1/2 teaspoon paprika
- » 200 ml coconut milk
- » 2 tablespoons extra virgin olive oil
- » salt and pepper to taste

Preparation:

1. Cut the chicken breast into cubes and finely chop the onion and bell bell pepper.
2. In a skillet, brown the onion and bell bell pepper with extra virgin olive oil.
3. Add the chicken breast and brown it on both sides.
4. Add the curry powder, paprika, salt, and pepper and mix well.
5. Pour in the coconut milk and bring to a boil.
6. Transfer to the basket of the air fryer oven.
7. Bake at 180°C for about 15 to 20 minutes, or until chicken is 100 percent cooked.
8. Serve the chicken curry hot.

Nutrition per portion: Calories: 500 kcal - Protein: 33 g - Fat: 37 g - Carbohydrates: 11 g – Fiber: 2.5 g – Sugars: 7.5 g

Preheat the Skillet: Ensure the skillet is hot before adding the oil and vegetables. This helps in achieving a good sear and better caramelization of the onions and bell peppers.

Adjust Spice Levels: If you prefer a spicier curry, add more curry powder or include a pinch of cayenne pepper. For a milder flavor, reduce the amount of curry powder.

Simmer for Richer Flavor: If you have extra time, let the curry simmer in the coconut milk for a few extra minutes before transferring to the air fryer. This helps meld the flavors together for a richer taste.

By following these tips, you'll enjoy a delicious and flavorful chicken curry that's easy to prepare and cook using your air fryer. Enjoy your meal!

36. SPICY CHICKEN WINGS

Ingredients:

- 8 chicken wings
- 2 tablespoons soy sauce
- 1 tablespoon honey

- 1/2 teaspoon paprika
- 1/2 teaspoon chili powder
- salt and pepper to taste

Preparation:

1. In a bowl, mix soy sauce, honey, paprika, chili powder, salt and pepper.
2. Add the chicken wings to the marinade and mix well.
3. Transfer the chicken wings to the basket of the air fryer oven.
4. Bake at 200°C for about 20-25 minutes, or until chicken wings are golden brown and 100 percent cooked through.
5. Serve the hot chicken wings hot.

Nutrition per portion: 360 kcal- Protein: 25 g - Fat: 22 g - Carbohydrates: 11 g – Fiber: 1 g – Sugars: 9 g

Marinate for Flavor: For more intense flavor, marinate the chicken wings in the soy sauce, honey, paprika, chili powder, salt, and pepper mixture for at least 30 minutes before cooking. This allows the flavors to penetrate the chicken, resulting in a more delicious dish.

Crispier Skin: For extra crispy chicken wings, pat them dry with paper towels before marinating. This helps remove excess moisture from the surface, allowing the skin to crisp up nicely in the air fryer. Additionally, halfway through cooking, turn the chicken wings to ensure even browning on all sides.

By following these tips, you'll enhance the flavor and texture of your chicken wings, creating a mouthwatering dish that's perfect for any occasion. Enjoy your hot and flavorful chicken wings straight from the air fryer!

37. GRILLED CHICKEN WITH BARBECUE SAUCE

Prep + Cook time: 35 min | **Serving:** 2 People

Ingredients:

» 2 chicken breasts
» 4 tablespoons barbecue sauce
» 2 tablespoons extra virgin olive oil
» salt and pepper to taste

Preparation:

1. Brush chicken breasts with extra virgin olive oil and season with salt and pepper to taste.
2. Transfer the chicken breasts to the basket of the air fryer oven.
3. Bake at 200°C for about 20-25 minutes, turning the chicken halfway through cooking.
4. Brush the chicken breasts with barbecue sauce and bake for another 5-10 minutes until golden brown and 100 percent cooked through.
5. Serve the grilled chicken with barbecue sauce hot.

Nutrition per portion: Calories: 380 kcal - Protein: 37g - Fat: 18g - Carbohydrates: 15g - Fiber: 0g - Sugars: 12g

Preheat for Even Cooking: Preheat your air fryer at 200°C for about 3-5 minutes before adding the chicken breasts. This ensures that the chicken starts cooking immediately and helps in achieving even cooking throughout.

Baste for Flavor: While cooking, baste the chicken breasts with barbecue sauce every 5-7 minutes using a brush or spoon. This helps in building layers of flavor and creates a delicious caramelized coating on the chicken.

By following these tips, you'll ensure that your grilled chicken breasts are perfectly cooked, flavorful, and have a tantalizing barbecue glaze that's sure to impress. Enjoy your hot and savory grilled chicken straight from the air fryer!

38. CHICKEN STRACCETTI WITH RUCOLA AND TOMATOES

Prep + Cook time: 30 min | **Serving:** 2 People

Ingredients:

» 2 chicken breasts
» 70 g arugula
» 150 g cherry tomatoes

» 2 tablespoons of extra virgin olive oil
» salt and pepper to taste

Preparation:

1. Cut chicken breasts into thin strips and season with extra virgin olive oil, salt and pepper.
2. Transfer the chicken breasts to the basket of the air fryer oven.
3. Bake at 200°C for about 20-25 minutes, turning the chicken halfway through cooking.
4. In a bowl, mix arugula and cherry tomatoes, and season with extra virgin olive oil, salt and pepper.
5. Serve the chicken strips with arugula and cherry tomatoes hot.

Nutrition per portion: Calories: 340 kcal- Protein: 38- Fat: 18 g- Carbohydrates: 3,5 g – Fiber: 1 g – Sugars: 2,5 g

Marinate for Flavor: Marinate the chicken breast strips in extra virgin olive oil, salt, and pepper for at least 15-20 minutes before cooking. This allows the flavors to infuse into the chicken, resulting in a more flavorful dish.

Optimal Cooking: Ensure the chicken strips are spread out evenly in the air fryer basket to allow for proper air circulation and even cooking. Avoid overcrowding the basket, as this can lead to unevenly cooked chicken.

By following these tips, you'll create tender and juicy chicken straccetti with vibrant arugula and cherry tomatoes, making for a delicious and satisfying meal! Enjoy the burst of flavors in every bite!

39. BAKED CHICKEN WITH SPICES

Prep + Cook time: 40 min | **Serving:** 2 People

Ingredients:

» 2 chicken thighs
» 1 teaspoon paprika
» 1 teaspoon cumin

» 1 teaspoon garlic powder
» 2 tablespoons extra virgin olive oil
» salt and pepper to taste

Preparation:

1. In a bowl, mix paprika, cumin, garlic powder, salt and pepper.
2. Brush the chicken thighs with extra virgin olive oil and sprinkle with the spice mixture.
3. Transfer the chicken thighs to the basket of the air fryer oven.
4. Bake at 200°C for about 20-25 minutes, or until the chicken is golden brown and 100 percent cooked through.
5. Serve the baked chicken with spices hot.

Nutrition per portion: Calories: 320 kcal- Protein: 23 g - Fat: 22 g - Carbohydrates: 3 g – Fiber: 0.75 g – Sugars: 0 g

Even Spice Distribution: Ensure the spice mixture is evenly distributed over the chicken thighs by rubbing it in thoroughly. This ensures that each bite is flavorful and well-seasoned.

Internal Temperature: Use a meat thermometer to check the internal temperature of the chicken thighs. They should reach an internal temperature of 75°C (165°F) to ensure they are fully cooked and safe to eat.

By following these tips, you'll create deliciously seasoned baked chicken thighs that are tender, flavorful, and perfectly cooked every time! Enjoy the aromatic blend of spices in this satisfying dish!

40. GRILLED CHICKEN WITH GRILLED VEGETABLES

Prep + Cook time: 10 min | **Serving:** 2 People

Ingredients:

»   2 chicken breasts
»   1 zucchini
»   1 bell bell pepper

»   1 eggplant
»   2 tablespoons extra virgin olive oil
»   salt and pepper to taste

Preparation:

1. Slice vegetables thinly and season with extra virgin olive oil, salt and pepper.
2. Brush chicken breasts with extra virgin olive oil and season with salt and pepper to taste.
3. Transfer the vegetables and chicken breasts to the basket of the air fryer oven.
4. Bake at 200°C for about 15-20 minutes, turning the vegetables and chicken halfway through cooking.
5. Serve the grilled chicken with grilled vegetables hot.

Nutrition per portion: Calories: 360 kcal - Protein: 46 g - Fat: 18 g - Carbohydrates: 13.5 g – Fiber: 3.5 g – Sugars: 6.5 g

Uniform Slicing: Ensure the vegetables are thinly sliced and of uniform thickness to ensure they cook evenly. This will prevent some pieces from being undercooked while others are overcooked.

Proper Seasoning: Season both the vegetables and chicken breasts generously with salt, pepper, and extra virgin olive oil. This enhances their flavor and helps them develop a delicious crust when grilled.

By following these tips, you'll create a perfectly grilled dish with tender chicken breasts and flavorful vegetables that are cooked to perfection. Enjoy the vibrant colors and delicious flavors of this healthy meal!

41. CHICKEN WITH MUSHROOMS AND PANNA

Prep + Cook time: 40 min | **Serving:** 2 People

Ingredients:

» 2 chicken breasts
» 150 g champignon mushrooms
» 1 onion
» 1 clove of garlic

» 100 ml cooking cream
» 2 tablespoons of extra virgin olive oil
» salt and pepper to taste

Preparation:

1. Cut chicken breasts into cubes and season with extra virgin olive oil, salt and pepper.
2. Transfer the chicken cubes to the basket of the air fryer oven.
3. Bake at 200°C for about 25-30 minutes, turning the chicken halfway through cooking.
4. Meanwhile, thinly slice the onion and mince the garlic.
5. In a skillet, heat a tablespoon of extra virgin olive oil and add the chopped onion and garlic. Cook over medium heat until the onion becomes translucent.
6. Add the sliced champignon mushrooms to the skillet and cook for about 5-7 minutes until they are soft.
7. Add the cream to the skillet and stir well.
8. Transfer the cooked chicken from the air fryer oven basket to the pan with the mushrooms and cream. Stir well and cook for another 2-3 minutes until the chicken is completely covered with the sauce.
9. Serve the chicken with mushrooms and cream hot.

Nutrition per portion: Calories: 507 kcal- Protein: 48 g- Fat: 33 g- Carbohydrates: 9 g – Fiber: 2 g – Sugars: 5 g

Even Cooking: Ensure the chicken breasts are cut into uniform cubes to promote even cooking. This will help prevent some pieces from drying out while others remain undercooked.

Creamy Sauce: To achieve a rich and creamy sauce, sauté the onions and garlic until they are soft and fragrant before adding the mushrooms. Cooking the mushrooms until they are golden brown adds depth of flavor to the dish. Finally, adding the cream and allowing it to simmer gently will thicken the sauce and infuse it with all the delicious flavors.

By following these tips, you'll create a delectable chicken dish with a creamy mushroom sauce that pairs perfectly with the tender chicken cubes. Enjoy this comforting and flavorful meal!

BEEF AND LAMB RECIPES

42. BEEF FILET WITH GREEN PEPPER

Prep + Cook time: 30 min | **Serving:** 2 People

Ingredients:

» 2 beef tenderloins (about 200 g each)
» 1 tablespoon green peppercorns
» 1/2 teaspoon salt
» 1 tablespoon olive oil

Preparation:

1. Crush the green peppercorns with a mortar or blender.
2. Add the salt and mix well.
3. Spread the pepper and salt mixture on the beef tenderloins.
4. Turn on the Breville Smart Pro air fryer and set the temperature to 200°C.
5. Place the fillets in the air fryer and cook for about 12 to 15 minutes for medium-rare, or longer depending on the desired degree of cooking.
6. Serve the beef tenderloins hot with vegetable garnishes to taste.

Nutrition per portion: - Calories: 367 kcal- Protein: 50 g- Fats: 17 g- Carbohydrates: 1 g – Fiber: 0.5 g – Sugars: 0.5 g

Seasoning Perfection: Ensure the green peppercorns are properly crushed to release their flavor. You can adjust the amount of salt according to your taste preference. Rub the pepper and salt mixture evenly onto the beef tenderloins, ensuring every part is seasoned for maximum flavor.

Temperature Control: For a perfectly cooked beef fillet, it's essential to monitor the cooking temperature. Aim for 200°C to achieve a nice sear on the outside while keeping the inside tender and juicy. Remember to adjust the cooking time based on your preferred level of doneness, whether it's medium-rare or medium-well.

By following these tips, you'll create a delicious beef fillet with a flavorful green pepper crust that's sure to impress. Enjoy this elegant dish paired with your favorite vegetable garnishes for a delightful meal!

43. ROAST OF BEEF WITH POTATOES

Prep + Cook time: 50 min | **Serving:** 2 People

Ingredients:

» 400 g beef roast
» 2 medium potatoes, peeled and diced
» 1 onion, chopped
» 2 cloves of garlic, minced

» 1/2 teaspoon salt
» 1/4 teaspoon black pepper
» 1 tablespoon olive oil

Preparation:

1. Turn on the Breville Smart Pro air fryer and set the temperature to 180°C (350°F).
2. In a bowl, mix the potatoes, onion, garlic, salt, pepper, and olive oil.
3. Place the beef roast in the air fryer and arrange the potatoes around it.
4. Cook for about 40 minutes, or until the roast has reached the desired internal temperature (60°C for medium-rare, 65°C for medium-rare, 70°C for medium-well cooked).
5. Remove the roast from the air fryer and let it rest for 10 minutes before slicing.
6. Serve the roast hot with the potatoes and vegetable garnishes to taste.

Nutrition per portion: Calories: 575 kcal- Protein: 47 g - Fat: 27 g - Carbohydrates: 30 g - Fiber: 4 g – Sugars: 4 g

Even Cooking: To ensure even cooking, make sure the potatoes are cut into uniform-sized pieces. This helps them cook evenly and prevents some pieces from being undercooked while others are overcooked. Mixing them with onion, garlic, salt, pepper, and olive oil not only adds flavor but also helps them cook evenly and become crispy on the outside.

Temperature Monitoring: Use a meat thermometer to check the internal temperature of the beef roast to achieve the desired level of doneness. The recommended temperatures provided ensure the roast is cooked to your preference, whether it's medium-rare, medium, or medium-well. Letting the roast rest after cooking allows the juices to redistribute, resulting in juicier and more flavorful meat.

By following these tips, you'll create a delicious roast beef dish with perfectly cooked potatoes, making it a satisfying and hearty meal for any occasion!

44. SKEWERS OF BEEF AND VEGETABLES

Prep + Cook time: 25 min | **Serving:** 2 People

Ingredients:

- » 300 g beef tenderloin, diced
- » 1 red bell bell pepper, diced
- » 1 red onion, diced
- » 8 cherry tomatoes
- » 1 tablespoon olive oil

- » 1/2 teaspoon salt
- » 1/4 teaspoon black pepper
- » 1/2 teaspoon dried oregano
- » 8 skewer sticks

Preparation:

1. Turn on the fryer and set the temperature to 200°C.
2. In a bowl, mix the olive oil, salt, black pepper, and dried oregano.
3. Thread the beef cubes, bell bell pepper, onion, and cherry tomatoes alternately on skewer sticks.
4. Brush the skewers with the oil and spice sea-soning.
5. Place the skewers in the air fryer and cook for about 10-12 minutes, turning them half-way through cooking, until the meat is golden brown and cooked through.
6. Serve the skewers hot with vegetable garnishes to taste.

Nutrition per portion: Calories: 405 kcal- Protein: 47 g- Fat: 16 g- Carbohydrates: 14 g - Fiber: 2.5 g – Sugars: 8 g

Marinate for Flavor: For a boost of flavor, consider marinating the beef cubes in the olive oil, salt, black pepper, and dried oregano mixture for 30 minutes before threading them onto the skewers. This allows the flavors to penetrate the meat, resulting in a more flavorful dish.

Even Cooking: To ensure even cooking, dice the beef, bell pepper, and onion into uniform-sized pieces. This helps them cook evenly and prevents some pieces from being undercooked or over-cooked. Alternating the beef with the vegetables on the skewers ensures that they cook uniformly.

Prevent Stickiness: To prevent the skewers from sticking to the air fryer basket, you can lightly spray or brush the basket with oil before placing the skewers. This helps in easy flipping and prevents any potential sticking.

45. SLICED BEEF WITH ROCKET AND GRANA CHEESE

Prep + Cook time: 25 min | **Serving:** 2 People

Ingredients:

- » 2 slices of beef sirloin (about 200 g each)
- » 1 cup arugula
- » 1/4 cup of parmesan shavings
- » 1 tablespoon olive oil
- » 1/2 teaspoon salt
- » 1/4 teaspoon black pepper

Preparation:

1. Turn on the air fryer and set the temperature to 200°C.
2. Brush the beef slices with olive oil and sprinkle with salt and black pepper.
3. Place the beef slices in the air fryer and cook for about 10-12 minutes for medium-rare, or longer depending on the desired degree of cooking.
4. Remove the beef slices from the air fryer and let them rest for a few minutes.
5. Cut the beef slices into thin slices and arrange them on a serving platter.
6. Add the arugula and parmesan shavings on top of the beef.
7. Serve the sliced beef hot with vegetable garnishes to taste.

Nutrition per portion: Calories: 310 kcal- Protein: 35 g- Fat: 19 g- Carbohydrates: 1 g - Fiber: 0.25 g – Sugars: 0 g

Rest for Juiciness: After cooking, allow the beef slices to rest for a few minutes before slicing. This helps redistribute the juices, ensuring that each slice remains juicy and tender.

Thin Slices: When slicing the beef, aim for thin slices to enhance the texture and presentation of the dish. A sharp knife works best for achieving clean, uniform slices.

Dress with Flavor: Drizzle the assembled dish with a balsamic reduction or a simple vinaigrette made with olive oil and lemon juice to add an extra layer of flavor. This complements the richness of the beef and the peppery arugula.

By following these tips, you'll create a delightful dish of sliced beef with rocket and Grana cheese that's bursting with flavor and perfectly cooked every time!

46. BEEF STEW WITH VEGETABLES

Prep + Cook time: 50 min | **Serving:** 2 People

Ingredients:

- » 400 g beef cubes
- » 2 carrots, cut into rounds
- » 1 onion, chopped
- » 2 potatoes, peeled and diced
- » 2 cups of beef stock

- » 1/2 teaspoon salt
- » 1/4 teaspoon black pepper
- » 1/2 teaspoon dried thyme
- » 1 bay leaf
- » 1 tablespoon olive oil

Preparation:

1. Turn on the air fryer and set the temperature to 180°C (350°F).
2. In a bowl, mix the beef, carrots, onion, and potatoes.
3. Place the meat and vegetable mixture in the air fryer and cook for about 10 minutes, until the vegetables are soft and the meat is golden brown.
4. Add the meat stock, salt, black pepper, thyme, and bay leaf to the air fryer and mix well.
5. Close the lid of the air fryer and cook for about 30 minutes, or until the meat and vegetables are soft and cooked through.
6. Serve the beef stew hot with toast or vegetable side dishes to taste.

Nutrition per portion: Calories: 650 kcal- Protein: 45 g- Fat: 33 g- Carbohydrates: 49 g - Fiber: 6.5 g – Sugars: 7.5 g

Layer Flavors: Enhance the depth of flavor in your beef stew by browning the beef cubes before adding them to the air fryer. This step caramelizes the meat, adding richness and complexity to the dish.

Control Moisture: To prevent your stew from becoming too watery, ensure that the lid of the air fryer is tightly closed during cooking. This helps retain moisture and concentrates the flavors, resulting in a thicker and more flavorful stew.

47. LAMB COSTOLETS

Prep + Cook time: 20 min | **Serving:** 2 People

Ingredients:

» 4 lamb chops
» 1 tablespoon olive oil
» 1/2 teaspoon salt

» 1/4 teaspoon black pepper
» 1 clove of garlic, minced
» 1 tablespoon chopped fresh parsley

Preparation:

1. Turn on the Breville Smart Pro air fryer and set the temperature to 200°C.
2. Brush the lamb chops with olive oil and sprinkle with salt, black pepper, garlic, and chopped parsley.
3. Place the ribs in the air fryer and cook for about 8-10 minutes per side, or longer depending on the desired degree of doneness.
4. Remove the lamb chops from the air fryer and let them rest for a few minutes before serving.
5. Serve the lamb chops hot with vegetable garnishes to taste.

Nutrition per portion: Calories: 350 kcal- Protein: 28 g- Fat: 25 g- Carbohydrates: 1 g Fiber: 0 g – Sugars: 0 g

Marinate for Flavor: Consider marinating the lamb chops for a few hours before cooking them. You can create a marinade using olive oil, garlic, lemon juice, and herbs like rosemary or thyme. Marinating adds flavor and helps tenderize the meat, enhancing its taste and texture.

Rest Before Serving: After cooking, allow the lamb chops to rest for a few minutes before serving. This allows the juices to redistribute throughout the meat, resulting in juicier and more flavorful costolets. Tenting the chops loosely with foil during this resting period can help retain their warmth.

48. ROAST OF LAMB WITH ROSEMARY AND GARLIC

Prep + Cook time: 50 min | **Serving:** 2 People

Ingredients:

- » 500 g boneless, rolled leg of lamb
- » 3 cloves of garlic, minced
- » 2 sprigs of fresh rosemary
- » 1 tablespoon olive oil
- » 1/2 teaspoon salt
- » 1/4 teaspoon black pepper

Preparation:

1. Turn on the Breville Smart Pro air fryer and set the temperature to 180°C (350°F).
2. In a bowl, mix the minced garlic, rosemary leaves, olive oil, salt, and black pepper.
3. Spread this mixture evenly over the rolled leg of lamb.
4. Place the leg of lamb on the air fryer grill and cook for about 40-45 minutes, or until the internal temperature of the lamb reaches 60°C for medium-rare cooking, or 70°C for medium cooking.
5. Remove the leg of lamb from the air fryer and let it rest for about 10 minutes before slicing and serving.
6. Serve the lamb roast hot with sides of vegetables to taste.

Nutrition per portion: Calories: 490 kcal- Protein: 50 g- Fat: 30 g- Carbohydrates: 1 g - Fiber: 0 g – Sugars: 0 g

Proper Seasoning: Ensure that the minced garlic, rosemary, olive oil, salt, and black pepper are thoroughly mixed to create a cohesive seasoning paste. This paste should be generously spread over the entire surface of the rolled leg of lamb, ensuring that every bite is infused with flavor.

Monitor Internal Temperature: Use a meat thermometer to monitor the internal temperature of the lamb as it cooks. This ensures that you achieve your desired level of doneness, whether it's medium-rare or medium. For medium-rare lamb, aim for an internal temperature of around 60°C, while for medium, aim for around 70°C. Allow the lamb to rest after cooking to allow the juices to redistribute, resulting in a more tender and flavorful roast.

49. PIZZAIOLA MEAT

Prep + Cook time: 35 min | **Serving:** 4 People

Ingredients:

- » 600 g beef steak cut into thin slices
- » 1 onion cut into thin slices
- » 2 cloves of garlic, minced
- » 400 g peeled tomatoes

- » 1 tablespoon dried oregano
- » 1 tablespoon chopped fresh basil
- » 2 tablespoons olive oil
- » Salt and pepper to taste

Preparation:

1. Turn on the Breville Smart Pro air fryer oven and set the temperature to 200°C.
2. In a frying pan, heat the olive oil and add the onion and garlic. Cook for a few minutes until soft.
3. Add the peeled tomatoes, oregano, basil, salt, and pepper to taste to the pan and mix well.
4. Cook the sauce for about 10 minutes, or until slightly thickened.
5. Arrange the beefsteak slices in a single layer in the basket of the air fryer oven.
6. Pour the tomato sauce over the meat.
7. Cook the meat pizzaiola in the air fryer oven for about 15-20 minutes, or until the meat is cooked to the desired doneness.
8. Remove the meat pizzaiola from the air fryer oven and serve hot.

Nutrition per portion: - Calories: 320 kcal- Protein: 32 g- Fats: 16 g- Carbohydrates: 7 g Fiber: 1.5 g – Sugars: 4 g

Thin Slices: Ensure that the beef steak is thinly sliced to allow for quick and even cooking in the air fryer oven. Thin slices will also absorb the flavors of the tomato sauce more effectively, resulting in a delicious and well-seasoned dish.

Even Distribution of Sauce: When arranging the beefsteak slices in the air fryer basket, ensure that they are spread out in a single layer. Pour the tomato sauce evenly over the meat to ensure that each slice is coated with the flavorful sauce. This will help prevent any dry spots and ensure a consistent taste throughout the dish.

50. BEEF HAMBURGER WITH BACON AND CHEESE

Prep + Cook time: 25 min | **Serving:** 2 People

Ingredients:

» 400 g ground beef
» 4 slices of bacon
» 2 slices of cheddar cheese

» 2 hamburger buns
» Lettuce, tomato and onion to taste
» Salt and pepper to taste

Preparation:

1. Turn on the Breville Smart Pro air fryer oven and set the temperature to 200°C.
2. Divide the beef into four equal parts and form four hamburgers.
3. Season the burgers with salt and pepper to taste.
4. Place the burgers in the basket of the air fryer oven and cook for about 12 to 15 minutes, turning them halfway through cooking, or until cooked to the desired doneness.
5. Meanwhile, cook bacon slices in a skillet until crispy.
6. Place a slice of cheddar cheese on top of each burger and melt for about one minute.
7. Cut the buns in half and place a lettuce leaf, a slice of tomato, and a slice of onion on each half.
8. Place the burgers with cheese on top of the bottom of the buns and top with a slice of bacon.
9. Close the buns and serve the beef burgers with bacon and cheese.

Nutrition per portion: - Calories: 610 kcal- Protein: 44 g- Fats: 39 g- Carbohydrates: 40 g - Fiber: 2 g – Sugars: 3 g

Create Indentations: Before cooking, press your thumb gently into the center of each hamburger patty to create a shallow indentation. This helps the patties cook evenly and prevents them from bulging up in the middle as they cook.

Bacon Placement: When assembling your burgers, consider placing the crispy bacon slices on top of the melted cheese. This not only adds a visually appealing layer to your burger but also prevents the bacon from sliding off while eating, ensuring each bite is flavorful and satisfying.

51. LAMB STEW WITH CARROTS AND PEAS

Prep + Cook time: 2 hours | **Serving:** 4 People

Ingredients:

» 800 g lamb cut into cubes
» 1 onion, chopped
» 2 carrots cut into rounds
» 2 cups fresh or frozen peas
» 2 tablespoons flour
» 2 tablespoons olive oil

» 2 cups chicken broth
» 1 cup dry red wine
» 2 tablespoons tomato paste
» 2 sprigs of fresh rosemary
» Salt and pepper to taste

Preparation:

1. Turn on the Breville Smart Pro air fryer oven and set the temperature to 180°C (350°F).
2. In a bowl, mix the lamb meat with the flour, salt and pepper.
3. In a saucepan, heat the olive oil and add the onion. Cook for a few minutes until soft.
4. Add the lamb and cook until golden brown on all sides.
5. Add the carrots, peas, chicken broth, red wine, tomato paste and rosemary. Stir well.
6. Transfer the mixture to an ovenproof dish and bake in the air fryer for about 2 hours, or until the lamb is tender and the sauce has thickened.
7. Remove the dish from the air fryer oven and serve the lamb stew with carrots and peas hot.

Nutrition per portion: - Calories: 560 kcal- Protein: 37 g- Fats: 25 g- Carbohydrates: 27 g - Fiber: 7 g – Sugars: 11 g

Flour Coating: Coating the lamb cubes in flour before cooking helps to thicken the stew as it cooks, resulting in a richer and heartier texture. Additionally, it helps the lamb pieces develop a golden-brown crust when searing, adding depth of flavor to the dish.

Slow Cooking: Slow cooking your lamb stew in the air fryer oven for about 2 hours allows the flavors to meld together and the meat to become incredibly tender. This low and slow-method ensures that the lamb is cooked to perfection and results in a deliciously flavorful stew. Make sure to check the stew occasionally and stir it gently to prevent sticking and ensure even cooking.

PORK RECIPES

52. PORK ROAST WITH POTATOES

Prep + Cook time: 1 hour 30 min | **Serving:** 2 People

Ingredients:

- » 400 g pork roast
- » 4 medium-sized potatoes
- » 2 tablespoons olive oil
- » 1 tablespoon chopped fresh rosemary

- » 1/2 tablespoon chopped fresh sage
- » 1/2 teaspoon salt
- » 1/4 teaspoon black pepper

Preparation:

1. Turn on the Breville Smart Pro air fryer oven and set the temperature to 200°C.
2. Cut the potatoes into cubes and place them in a bowl. Add 1 tablespoon of olive oil, salt, and black pepper and mix well.
3. In a skillet, heat 1 tablespoon olive oil and brown the pork loin on all sides.
4. Brush the pork loin with the chopped rosemary and sage.
5. Place the pork loin and potatoes on the grill of the air fryer oven and bake for about 1 hour and 15 minutes, or until the internal temperature of the pork loin reaches 65°C.
6. Remove the pork arista and potatoes from the air fryer oven and let them rest for a few minutes before slicing the arista and serving.

Nutrition per portion: Calories: 690 kcal - Protein: 28 g - Fats: 30 g - Carbohydrates: 45 g Fiber: 4 g – Sugars: 4 g

Even Slicing: When slicing the pork roast after cooking, aim for uniform slices to ensure that each portion is evenly cooked and tender. This also enhances the presentation of the dish.

Internal Temperature: To guarantee that the pork loin is cooked perfectly, use a meat thermometer to check its internal temperature. The recommended safe internal temperature for pork is 65°C (145°F). Insert the thermometer into the thickest part of the meat to get an accurate reading. If you prefer your pork to be more well-done, you can cook it to a higher temperature, but be careful not to overcook it to maintain its tenderness and juiciness.

53. PORK RIBS

Prep + Cook time: 25 min | **Serving:** 2 People

Ingredients:

- » 4 pork chops
- » 1 tablespoon olive oil
- » 1/2 teaspoon salt
- » 1/4 teaspoon black pepper
- » 1/2 teaspoon sweet paprika

Preparation:

1. Turn on the air fryer oven and set the temperature to 200°C.
2. In a bowl, mix the salt, black pepper, and sweet paprika.
3. Brush the pork chops with olive oil and sprinkle with the prepared spice mixture.
4. Place the ribs on the air fryer oven rack and cook for about 15 to 20 minutes, turning them halfway through cooking, or until well cooked and crispy.
5. Serve the pork chops hot, accompanied by a side of vegetables to taste.

Nutrition per portion: Calories: 290 kcal- Protein: 27 g- Fat: 16 g- Carbohydrates: 1 g -Fiber: 0 g – Sugars: 0 g

Marinating Time: Consider marinating the pork chops for a few hours or overnight before cooking. This allows the flavors to penetrate the meat, resulting in a more flavorful dish. You can use a marinade of your choice, such as a mixture of soy sauce, garlic, honey, and Worcestershire sauce, to infuse the pork chops with delicious flavors.

Broil for Crispiness: After air frying the pork chops, you can further enhance their texture by broiling them for a few minutes. This will help crisp up the exterior, giving the ribs a delightful crunch. Simply transfer the cooked pork chops to a baking sheet and broil them in the oven on high heat for 2-3 minutes until they reach your desired level of crispiness. Keep an eye on them to prevent burning.

54. PORK TENDERLOIN IN BACON CRUST

Prep + Cook time: 40 min | **Serving:** 2 People

Ingredients:

» 2 pork tenderloins
» 6 slices of bacon
» 1 tablespoon Dijon mustard

» 1 tablespoon honey
» 1/2 teaspoon salt
» 1/4 teaspoon black pepper

Preparation:

1. Turn on the air fryer oven and set the temperature to 200°C.
2. In a bowl, mix Dijon mustard, honey, salt, and black pepper.
3. Spread the mustard and honey mixture on the pork tenderloins.
4. Wrap each pork tenderloin with 3 slices of bacon, making sure the bacon completely covers the tenderloins.
5. Place the pork tenderloins on the air fryer oven rack and bake for about 25-30 minutes, or until the internal temperature of the tenderloins reaches 65°C.
6. Remove the pork tenderloins from the air fryer oven and let them rest for a few minutes before slicing and serving.

Nutrition per portion: Calories: 400 kcal- Protein: 42 g- Fat: 20 g- Carbohydrates: 9 g - Fiber: 0 g – Sugars: 9.5 g

Secure Bacon Wrapping: When wrapping the pork tenderloins with bacon, make sure to secure the bacon slices firmly around the tenderloins. This will prevent them from unraveling during cooking and ensure that the bacon forms a crispy crust around the meat. You can use toothpicks to secure the ends of the bacon slices if needed.

Use a Meat Thermometer: To ensure that the pork tenderloins are cooked to perfection without overcooking, use a meat thermometer to check the internal temperature. Insert the thermometer into the thickest part of the tenderloins, away from any bone or fat. The pork is done when it reaches an internal temperature of 65°C. This will help you achieve juicy and tender pork tenderloins every time.

55. SKEWERS OF PIGS AND PINEAPPLES

Prep + Cook time: 30 min | **Serving:** 2 People

Ingredients:

» 300 g diced pork
» 1/2 diced fresh pineapple
» 1 tablespoon olive oil
» 1/2 teaspoon salt
» 1/4 teaspoon black pepper
» 1/2 teaspoon sweet paprika
» 4 skewer sticks

Preparation:

1. Turn on the Breville Smart Pro air fryer oven and set the temperature to 200°C.
2. In a bowl, mix the olive oil, salt, black pepper, and sweet paprika.
3. Thread them alternately onto the 4 skewer sticks, starting with the pork and ending with the pineapple.
4. Place the skewers on the air fryer oven rack and cook for about 15-20 minutes, turning them halfway through cooking, until the pork is well cooked and the pineapple is golden brown.
5. Serve the pork and pineapple skewers hot, accompanied by a sauce to taste.

Nutrition per portion: Calories: 250 kcal- Protein: 22 g- Fat: 10 g- Carbohydrates: 21 g - Fiber: 1 g – Sugars: 8 g

Evenly-Sized Pieces: Ensure that the pork and pineapple pieces are cut to similar sizes. This will help them cook evenly and prevent some pieces from being overcooked while others remain under-cooked. Aim for 1-inch cubes for both the pork and pineapple.

Pre-soak Skewer Sticks: If you are using wooden skewer sticks, soak them in water for at least 30 minutes before threading the pork and pineapple. This will prevent the sticks from burning or catching fire in the air fryer, ensuring a safer cooking process.

56. PORK STEW WITH MUSHROOMS AND POTATOES

Prep + Cook time: 1 hour 30 min | **Serving:** 2 People

Ingredients:

- » 400 g cubed pork
- » 200 g cubed potatoes
- » 200 g sliced champignon mushrooms
- » 1 onion, chopped
- » 2 cloves of garlic, minced
- » 1 tablespoon olive oil

- » 1/2 teaspoon salt
- » 1/4 teaspoon black pepper
- » 1/2 teaspoon dried thyme
- » 1/2 teaspoon dried rosemary
- » 500 ml vegetable broth

Preparation:

1. Turn on the Breville Smart Pro air fryer oven and set the temperature to 180°C (350°F).
2. In a bowl, mix the salt, black pepper, thyme, and rosemary.
3. In a saucepan, heat the olive oil and brown the onion and garlic until soft.
4. Add the pork and cook until golden brown.
5. Add the potatoes and mushrooms to the pot and mix well.
6. Add the prepared spice mix and vegetable broth and bring to a boil.
7. Transfer the contents of the pot to a baking dish and cover with a sheet of baking paper.
8. Place the dish on the air fryer oven rack and bake for about 1 hour, or until the pork and potatoes are soft and the liquid has reduced.
9. Remove the dish from the air fryer oven and serve the pork stew with mushrooms and potatoes hot.

Nutrition per portion: Calories: 370 kcal- Protein: 32 g- Fat: 14 g- Carbohydrates: 32 g - Fiber: 3 g – Sugars: 4 g

Stirring for Even Cooking: About halfway through the cooking time, carefully remove the baking dish from the air fryer and give the stew a good stir. This ensures that all ingredients cook evenly and helps the flavors meld together more harmoniously.

Using Fresh Herbs: For an extra burst of flavor, consider using fresh thyme and rosemary instead of dried. Simply add a few sprigs of fresh herbs to the stew before transferring it to the air fryer. Remove the sprigs before serving for a more vibrant and aromatic dish.

57. PIGEON BREAD WITH CARROTS AND SEDANES

Prep + Cook time: 50 min | **Serving:** 2 People

Ingredients:

» 400 g ground pork
» 1 egg
» 1/2 cup breadcrumbs
» 1/4 cup milk
» 1/2 onion, chopped
» 1/2 cup grated carrots

» 1/2 cup chopped celery
» 1 teaspoon dijon mustard
» 1 teaspoon English sauce
» 1/2 teaspoon salt
» 1/4 teaspoon black pepper

Preparation:

1. Turn on the Breville Smart Pro air fryer oven and set the temperature to 180°C (350°F).
2. In a bowl, mix ground pork, egg, bread crumbs, milk, onion, carrots, celery, Dijon mustard, English sauce, salt, and black pepper.
3. Transfer the mixture to a loaf pan and bake in the air fryer oven for about 35 to 40 minutes, or until the meatloaf is well cooked.
4. Remove the meatloaf from the air fryer oven and let it rest for a few minutes before cutting and serving.

Nutrition per portion: Calories: 550 kcal- Protein: 34 g- Fat: 35 g- Carbohydrates: 28 g – Fiber: 3 g -Sugars: 6.50 g

Avoid Overmixing: When combining the ingredients for the meatloaf, mix just until everything is well combined. Overmixing can make the meatloaf dense and tough. Using a gentle touch will result in a more tender and moist meatloaf.

Check Internal Temperature: To ensure the meatloaf is thoroughly cooked, use a meat thermometer to check the internal temperature. The meatloaf should reach an internal temperature of 75°C (165°F). If the top is browning too quickly, you can cover it with aluminum foil for the last 10-15 minutes of cooking to prevent burning.

58. PORK CURRY WITH BASED RICE

Ingredients:

»   300 g pork cut into cubes
»   1 chopped onion
»   1 red bell pepper cut into cubes
»   1 yellow bell pepper cut into cubes
»   2 tablespoons of curry paste
»   1 cup of coconut milk

»   1 cup of chicken broth
»   1 cup basmati rice
»   2 cups water
»   Salt and pepper to taste
»   Olive oil to taste

Preparation:

1. Heat the olive oil in a large skillet and add the onion, peppers and pork. Cook for a few minutes until golden brown.
2. Add the curry paste and stir well to distribute it evenly.
3. Add the coconut milk and chicken broth, season with salt and pepper to taste. Allow to cook for about 20-25 minutes, or until pork is well cooked.
4. Meanwhile, in another pot, bring the water to a boil and add the basmati rice. Cover and cook for about 18-20 minutes, or until the rice is soft and cooked through.
5. Serve the pork curry with the hot basmati rice.

Nutrition per portion: Calories: 750 kcal- Protein: 32 g- Fat: 43 g- Carbohydrates: 91 g - Fiber: 4 g -Sugars: 7.5 g

Optimize Cooking Time: To speed up the process, cook the basmati rice in the air fryer while preparing the pork curry. Use a suitable air fryer-safe dish for the rice, and follow the same water-to-rice ratio. This way, both components will be ready at the same time, and you'll save on clean-up.

Enhance the Flavors: Before adding the curry paste, toast it in the skillet for about a minute until fragrant. This step will help to release the essential oils and deepen the flavor of the curry. Additionally, you can add a squeeze of fresh lime juice and a handful of chopped cilantro just before serving to brighten up the dish and add a fresh contrast to the rich curry.

59. ROAST PORK WITH POTATOES AND CARROTS

Prep + Cook time: 2 hour 30 min | **Serving:** 4-6 People

Ingredients:

- » 1 kg pork roast
- » 4 medium-sized potatoes cut into cubes
- » 4 carrots cut into cubes
- » 1 onion chopped
- » 2 cloves of garlic, chopped
- » 2 tablespoons olive oil

- » 1 cup of chicken broth
- » 1/2 cup dry white wine
- » 1 teaspoon chopped rosemary
- » 1 teaspoon chopped thyme
- » Salt and pepper to taste

Preparation:

1. Preheat oven to 180°C (350°F).
2. In a large skillet, heat the olive oil and brown the pork roast on all sides until golden brown. Transfer it to a baking sheet.
3. Add the potatoes, carrots, onion, and garlic around the roast and mix well.
4. Add the chicken broth, white wine, rosemary, thyme, salt, and pepper. Cover the roasting pan with aluminum foil and bake in the oven for about 2 hours.
5. Remove the aluminum foil and bake for another 30 minutes, or until the potatoes and carrots are soft and the roast is well cooked.
6. Remove the roasting pan from the oven and let the roast rest for about 10 minutes before slicing and serving with the baked potatoes and carrots.

Nutrition per portion: Calories: 545 kcal - Protein: 29 g - Fats: 32 g - Carbohydrates: 36 g - Fiber: 5 g -Sugars: 4 g

Even Cooking: Cut the potatoes and carrots into uniform pieces to ensure even cooking. Since the air fryer circulates hot air around the food, uniformity in size will help the vegetables cook at the same rate as the pork. Also, consider giving the vegetables a head start by cooking them for 10 minutes in the air fryer before adding the browned pork roast.

Flavor Infusion: To enhance the flavor, marinate the pork roast with rosemary, thyme, garlic, salt, pepper, and a tablespoon of olive oil for a few hours or overnight. This allows the herbs and spices to penetrate the meat, resulting in a more flavorful roast. Additionally, basting the roast with the chicken broth and wine mixture periodically during cooking will keep the meat moist and infuse it with even more flavor.

60. STEWED PIG WITH BEANS

Prep + Cook time: 1 hour 30 min | **Serving:** 4 People

Ingredients:

- » 500 g pork cut into cubes
- » 1 onion, chopped
- » 2 cloves of garlic, minced
- » 2 tablespoons olive oil
- » 2 cups drained cooked borlotti beans

- » 1 cup of tomato puree
- » 1 cup of chicken broth
- » 1 teaspoon dried oregano
- » Salt and pepper to taste

Preparation:

1. Turn on the Breville Smart Pro air fryer oven and set the temperature to 180°C (350°F).
2. In a large pot, heat the olive oil and add the onion and garlic. Cook for a few minutes until soft.
3. Add the pork and cook until golden brown on all sides.
4. Add the borlotti beans, tomato puree, chicken broth, oregano, salt and pepper. Stir well.
5. Transfer the mixture to an ovenproof dish and bake in the air fryer for about 1 hour, or until the pork is tender and the sauce has thickened.
6. Remove the dish from the air fryer oven and serve the pork stew with beans hot.

Nutrition per portion: Calories: 400 kcal - Protein: 32 g - Fats: 12 g - Carbohydrates: 35 g - Fiber: 8.5 g -Sugars: 4.7 g

Layering Flavors: For richer flavors, consider marinating the pork cubes in a mixture of olive oil, garlic, oregano, salt, and pepper for at least an hour before cooking. This will allow the flavors to penetrate the meat, enhancing its taste. Additionally, sautéing the onion and garlic until golden brown before adding the pork will add depth to the dish.

Moisture Control: To prevent the pork from drying out during the cooking process, cover the ovenproof dish tightly with aluminum foil before placing it in the air fryer. This will help retain moisture and ensure that the pork remains juicy and tender. Additionally, periodically check the stew while it's cooking and add more chicken broth if necessary to maintain the desired consistency of the sauce.

61. PORK RIBS WITH TOMATO SALAD

Prep + Cook time: 30 min| **Serving:** 2 People

Ingredients:

- » 4 pork chops
- » 2 diced tomatoes
- » 1 red onion cut into thin slices
- » 1 cucumber cut into cubes

- » 1 diced ripe avocado
- » 2 tablespoons olive oil
- » 2 tablespoons white wine vinegar
- » Salt and pepper to taste

Preparation:

1. Turn on the Breville Smart Pro air fryer oven and set the temperature to 200°C.
2. Brush the pork chops with a little olive oil and season with salt and pepper to taste.
3. Grill the pork chops in the air fryer oven for about 10 to 12 minutes, or until well done.
4. Meanwhile, prepare the tomato salad. In a bowl, mix the tomatoes, red onion, cucumber, and avocado.
5. Dress the salad with olive oil, white wine vinegar, salt, and pepper to taste.
6. Serve the grilled pork chops with the tomato salad.

Nutrition per portion: Calories: 694 kcal, Protein: 43 g, Fats: 51 g, Carbohydrates: 17 g Fiber: 7.5 g -Sugars: 6 g

Optimal Pork Cooking: To ensure your pork chops are perfectly cooked, use a meat thermometer to check for doneness. Pork should reach an internal temperature of 145°F (63°C) for medium-rare and 160°F (71°C) for medium. Insert the thermometer into the thickest part of the chop to get an accurate reading.

Enhancing Tomato Salad: For added flavor and freshness, consider adding a squeeze of fresh lemon juice to the tomato salad dressing. The acidity will complement the richness of the pork and elevate the overall taste of the dish. Additionally, sprinkle some chopped fresh herbs like parsley or basil over the salad just before serving for a burst of freshness and color.

62. PORK SLICES WITH SENAPE

Prep + Cook time: 25 min | **Serving:** 4 People

Ingredients:

» 4 slices of pork
» 2 tablespoons Dijon mustard
» 2 tablespoons honey
» 1 tablespoon olive oil
» Salt and pepper to taste

Preparation:

1. Turn on the Breville Smart Pro air fryer oven and set the temperature to 200°C.
2. In a bowl, mix Dijon mustard, honey, olive oil, salt and pepper.
3. Brush the pork slices with the mustard and honey marinade.
4. Place the pork slices in the basket of the air fryer oven.
5. Bake the pork slices in the air fryer oven for about 15-20 minutes, or until cooked and golden brown.
6. Remove the pork slices from the air fryer oven and serve hot.

Nutrition per portion: Calories: 250 kcal, Protein: 26 g, Fats: 9 g, Carbohydrates: 13 g Fiber: 0 g -Sugars: 9 g

Marinating Time: For maximum flavor infusion, consider marinating the pork slices in the mustard and honey mixture for at least 30 minutes before cooking. This allows the flavors to penetrate the meat, resulting in a more flavorful and tender dish.

Crispy Finish: To achieve a crispy exterior on the pork slices, you can broil them for a few minutes after air frying. Simply switch the air fryer oven to the broil setting for the last 1-2 minutes of cooking, keeping a close eye to prevent burning. This extra step will add a delightful crunch to the dish while keeping the interior juicy and tender.

63. PORK SAUSAGES

Prep + Cook time: 20 min | **Serving:** 4 People

Ingredients:

»   8 pork sausages
»   1 tablespoon olive oil

»   Salt and pepper to taste

Preparation:

1. Turn on the Breville Smart Pro air fryer oven and set the temperature to 200°C.
2. Place the pork sausages in the basket of the air fryer oven.
3. Brush the pork sausages with olive oil and season with salt and pepper to taste.
4. Cook the pork sausages in the air fryer oven for about 15 to 20 minutes, turning them halfway through cooking, or until cooked through and golden brown.
5. Remove the pork sausages from the air fryer oven and serve hot.

Nutrition per portion: Calories: 325 kcal - Protein: 16 g - Fats: 28 g – Carbohydrates: 0 Fiber: 0 g -Sugars: 0 g

Preheat the Air Fryer Oven: Before starting the cooking process, preheat the air fryer oven to 200°C for about 3-5 minutes. This will ensure that the food begins cooking immediately upon insertion into the oven, reducing the overall cooking time and ensuring even heat distribution.

Use Skewers: For even crispier and more uniform cooking, skewer the sausages before placing them in the air fryer basket. This will allow the heat to circulate better around the sausages, ensuring an even browning on all sides. Make sure to turn the sausages halfway through cooking for a perfect result on all sides.

64. PORK PULPETS WITH SUGAR

Prep + Cook time: 40 min | **Serving:** 4 People

Ingredients:

- » 500 g ground pork
- » 1 egg
- » 1/2 cup breadcrumbs
- » 1/4 cup grated Parmesan cheese
- » 1/4 cup milk

- » 2 cloves of garlic, minced
- » 2 tablespoons chopped fresh parsley
- » 1 tablespoon olive oil
- » 400 g peeled tomatoes
- » Salt and pepper to taste

Preparation:

1. Turn on the Breville Smart Pro air fryer oven and set the temperature to 200°C.
2. In a bowl, mix ground pork, egg, breadcrumbs, grated Parmesan cheese, milk, garlic, parsley, salt and pepper to taste.
3. Form pork patties of the desired size and place them in the basket of the air fryer oven.
4. Bake the pork patties in the air fryer oven for about 20-25 minutes, or until golden brown.
5. Meanwhile, in a frying pan, heat the olive oil and add the peeled tomatoes. Cook for a few minutes until slightly thickened.
6. Add the pork meatballs to the sauce and cook for another 10-15 minutes.
7. Remove the pork meatballs with sauce from the air fryer oven and serve hot.

Nutrition per portion: Calories: 365 kcal - Protein: 30 g - Fats: 21 g - Carbohydrates: 38 g - Fiber: 1.5 g -Sugars: 4.5 g

Drain excess moisture from the ground pork: Before mixing the ingredients, pat the ground pork with paper towels to remove excess moisture. This will help the pork meatballs hold their shape better and prevent them from becoming too soggy during cooking.

Pre-cook the sauce: To enhance the flavor of the sauce and ensure it's thoroughly cooked, pre-cook it separately before adding the pork meatballs. This step allows the flavors to meld together and ensures the sauce reaches the desired consistency before combining it with the meatballs.

VEGETABLE AND VEGAN RECIPES

65. GRILLED VEGETABLE TACOS

Prep + Cook time: 20 min | **Serving:** 2 People

Ingredients:

» 1 red bell bell pepper
» 1 yellow bell bell pepper
» 1 zucchini
» 1 red onion
» 1 clove of garlic
» 1 tablespoon extra virgin olive oil
» 1 teaspoon smoked paprika
» 1/2 teaspoon cumin powder
» salt and pepper to taste
» 4 tortillas
» 1 ripe avocado
» a few cilantro leaves
» lime juice

Preparation:

1. Cut peppers, zucchini, and onion into thin slices. Chop the garlic.
2. Season vegetables with extra virgin olive oil, smoked paprika, cumin powder, salt, and pepper.
3. Transfer the seasoned vegetables to the basket of the air fryer oven. Bake at 200°C for about 10-12 minutes, turning the vegetables halfway through cooking.
4. Meanwhile, heat the tortillas in a frying pan or air fryer oven for a few minutes until they are hot and soft.
5. Cut avocado into cubes and season with lime juice and salt.
6. Assemble the tacos: place the grilled vegetables on the tortilla, add the avocado and a few cilantro leaves.
7. Repeat the process with the other tortillas and serve hot.

Nutrition per portion: Calories: 400 kcal - Protein: 9 g - Fat: 22 g - Carbohydrates: 65 g - Fiber: 12 g -Sugars: 10 g

Evenly slice the vegetables: To ensure that the vegetables cook evenly and quickly, make sure to slice them into thin and uniform pieces. This will help them cook through evenly and avoid any undercooked or overcooked pieces.

66. SESAME TOFU

Ingredients:

» 250 g tofu
» 2 tablespoons of soy sauce
» 1 tablespoon sesame oil
» 1 tablespoon of sesame seeds
» salt and pepper to taste

Preparation:

1. Cut tofu into cubes and season with soy sauce, sesame oil, salt, and pepper.
2. Transfer the seasoned tofu to the basket of the air fryer oven.
3. Bake the tofu at 200°C for about 10 to 12 minutes.
4. Sprinkle the tofu with sesame seeds and bake for another 2-3 minutes until the seeds are golden brown.
5. Serve the sesame tofu hot as a side dish or as an ingredient in salads or bowls.

Nutrition per portion: Calories: 170 kcal - Protein: 14 g - Fat: 10 g - Carbohydrates: 5 g - Fiber: 1.5 g -Sugars: 0 g

Press the tofu: Before cutting the tofu into cubes, it's beneficial to press it to remove excess moisture. Simply place the tofu block between paper towels or kitchen towels and place a heavy object on top, like a plate or a cast-iron skillet. Let it press for about 15-20 minutes. Pressing the tofu will help it absorb more flavor from the marinade and achieve a firmer texture when cooked.

Preheat the air fryer: To ensure that the tofu cooks evenly and gets crispy on the outside, preheat the air fryer oven for a few minutes before adding the seasoned tofu cubes. This step will create a hot environment right from the start, allowing the tofu to cook more efficiently and develop a nice golden crust.

67. VEGETABLE CASSEROLE

Prep + Cook time: 20 min | **Serving:** 2 People

Ingredients:

» 2 zucchini
» 1 carrot
» 1 onion
» 2 eggs

» 50 g grated cheese
» 1 tablespoon extra virgin olive oil
» salt and pepper to taste

Preparation:

1. Cut zucchini, carrot, and onion into thin slices.
2. In a skillet, heat a tablespoon of extra virgin olive oil and add the vegetables. Cook over medium heat for about 10-12 minutes until they are soft.
3. In a bowl, beat the eggs with the grated cheese, salt and pepper.
4. Add the vegetables to the bowl with the eggs and mix well.
5. Transfer the egg and vegetable mixture to an ovenproof dish or 2 flan molds.
6. Bake the vegetable flan in the air fryer oven at 180°C (350°F) for about 15-20 minutes until golden brown on the surface.
7. Serve the vegetable flan hot as a main dish or side dish.

Nutrition per portion: Calories: 250 kcal - Protein: 16 g - Fat: 18 g - Carbohydrates: 12 g - Fiber: 2.5 g -Sugars: 7 g

68. POTATO AND SPINACH CROQUETTES

Prep + Cook time: 30 min | **Serving:** 2 People

Ingredients:

» 2 medium potatoes
» 100 g fresh spinach
» 1/4 onion, chopped
» 50 g chickpea flour

» 1 egg
» 50 g breadcrumbs
» salt and pepper to taste
» olive oil extra virgin olive oil spray

Preparation:

1. Peel the potatoes and cut them into cubes. Cook them in salted boiling water until tender.
2. Meanwhile, blanch the spinach in boiling salted water for a few minutes and then drain.
3. In a skillet, sauté the chopped onion with a drizzle of extra virgin olive oil until soft.
4. Drain the potatoes and mash them with a fork or potato masher. Add the spinach and sautéed onion to the potatoes and mix well.
5. Form croquettes with your hands and dip them in chickpea flour, beaten egg, and bread crumbs.
6. Transfer the potato and spinach croquettes to the basket of the air fryer oven and bake at 180°C (350°F) for about 15-20 minutes until golden brown and crispy.
7. Serve the potato and spinach croquettes hot as a main dish or side dish.

Nutrition per portion: Calories: 350 kcal - Protein: 10 g - Fat: 9 g - Carbohydrates: 50 g - Fiber: 6.5 g -Sugars: 4.5 g

Ensure proper drainage of the spinach: After blanching the spinach, make sure to drain it thoroughly to remove excess moisture. Excess moisture can make the croquettes soggy and affect their texture. You can use a colander or paper towels to squeeze out the water from the spinach before adding it to the mashed potatoes.

Coat the croquettes evenly: When dipping the croquettes in chickpea flour, beaten egg, and breadcrumbs, ensure they are evenly coated on all sides. This will help create a crispy and golden exterior when baked in the air fryer oven. Take your time to coat each croquette thoroughly before transferring them to the air fryer basket for cooking.

69. BAKED STUFFED MUSHROOMS AIR FRYER

Prep + Cook time: 20 min | **Serving:** 2 People

Ingredients:

» 4 large button mushrooms
» 1/4 onion, chopped
» 1 clove of garlic, minced
» 1/4 cup breadcrumbs

» 1/4 cup grated cheese
» 1 tablespoon chopped parsley
» 1 tablespoon extra virgin olive oil
» salt and pepper to taste

Preparation:

1. Remove the stems of the mushrooms and drain the middle part.
2. In a pan, sauté the onion and garlic with a tablespoon of extra virgin olive oil until soft.
3. Add the breadcrumbs, grated cheese, parsley, salt, and pepper to the pan and mix well.
4. Fill the mushrooms with the breadcrumb and cheese mixture.
5. Transfer the stuffed mushrooms to the basket of the air fryer oven.
6. Bake the stuffed mushrooms in the air fryer oven at 180°C for about 10-12 minutes until they are golden brown on the surface.
7. Serve the stuffed mushrooms hot as an appetizer or side dish.

Nutrition per portion: Calories: 210 kcal - Protein: 7 g - Fat: 7 g - Carbohydrates: 15 g - Fiber: 1.5 g -Sugars: 3 g

Pre-cook the filling: Before stuffing the mushrooms, consider pre-cooking the filling mixture on the stovetop for a few minutes. This will help to meld the flavors together and ensure that the breadcrumbs are nicely toasted. It will also reduce the moisture content of the filling, preventing the mushrooms from becoming soggy during baking.

Arrange mushrooms evenly in the air fryer basket: To ensure even cooking, arrange the stuffed mushrooms in a single layer in the air fryer basket without overcrowding. This allows for proper air circulation around each mushroom, resulting in evenly cooked and golden-brown mushrooms. If necessary, cook the mushrooms in batches to avoid overcrowding.

70. ARTICHOKES STUFFED

Prep + Cook time: 30 min | **Serving:** 2 People

Ingredients:

»   2 large artichokes
»   1/4 cup breadcrumbs
»   1/4 cup grated cheese
»   1 clove of garlic, minced
»   1 tablespoon chopped parsley
»   1/4 cup extra virgin olive oil
»   salt and pepper to taste

Preparation:

1.   Clean the artichokes by removing the tough outer leaves and inner hay.
2.   In a bowl, mix the breadcrumbs, grated cheese, minced garlic, parsley, salt, and pepper.
3.   Fill the center of the artichokes with the breadcrumb and cheese mixture.
4.   Transfer the stuffed artichokes to the basket of the air fryer oven.
5.   Spray the artichokes with extra virgin olive oil spray.
6.   Bake the stuffed artichokes in the air fryer oven at 180°C for about 20-25 minutes until they are golden brown on the surface.
7.   Serve the stuffed artichokes hot as an appetizer or side dish.

Nutrition per portion: Calories:413 kcal - Protein: 9 g - Fat: 31 g - Carbohydrates: 25 g - Fiber: 7.5 g -Sugars: 1.5 g

Pre-cook the artichokes: Since artichokes can be quite dense and fibrous, consider pre-cooking them partially before stuffing and air frying. Steam or boil the cleaned artichokes for about 15-20 minutes until they are slightly tender. This will help ensure that the artichokes cook through evenly and become tender during the air frying process.

Protect the exposed edges: Artichoke leaves can become dry and crispy during air frying. To prevent this, cover the exposed edges of the stuffed artichokes with aluminum foil. This will help retain moisture and ensure that the leaves remain tender while the filling cooks and the outer layers become golden brown. Remove the foil during the last few minutes of cooking to allow the surface to crisp up nicely.

71. KALE CHIPS

Prep + Cook time: 15 min | **Serving:** 2 People

Ingredients:

» 1 small kale
» 1 tablespoon extra virgin olive oil

» salt and pepper to taste

Preparation:

1. Wash and dry the kale leaves and cut them into pieces of about 2 inches.
2. Season the kale leaves with extra virgin olive oil, salt and pepper.
3. Transfer the kale leaves to the basket of the air fryer oven.
4. Bake the kale chips in the air fryer oven at 200°C for about 5-7 minutes until crispy.
5. Serve the kale chips as a healthy snack or side dish.

Nutrition per portion: Calories: 80 kcal - Protein: 2 g - Fat: 5 g - Carbohydrates: 7 g Fiber: 1.85 g -Sugars: 1 g

Massage the kale: Before seasoning and air frying, take a few minutes to massage the kale leaves with the olive oil. This helps to break down the tough fibers in the kale and evenly distribute the oil, resulting in crispier and more evenly cooked chips.

Check frequently: Keep an eye on the kale chips as they cook in the air fryer, as they can quickly go from perfectly crispy to burnt. Check them every few minutes and shake the basket if needed to ensure even cooking. Adjust the cooking time as necessary based on your air fryer's settings and the level of crispiness you prefer.

72. CHICKPEA AND SWEET POTATO MEATBALLS

Prep + Cook time: 45 min | **Serving:** 2 People

Ingredients:

- » 1 cup cooked chickpeas
- » 1 cup peeled and cooked sweet potatoes
- » 1 chopped onion
- » 2 cloves of garlic, minced
- » 1/4 cup chopped parsley
- » 1/2 cup breadcrumbs
- » 1 egg
- » 1 tablespoon extra virgin olive oil
- » Salt and pepper to taste

Preparation:

1. Turn on the air fryer oven to 180°C (350°F).
2. In a bowl, mash the chickpeas and sweet potatoes with a fork until smooth.
3. Add the onion, garlic, parsley, bread crumbs, and egg to the bowl and mix well.
4. Form the chickpea and sweet potato patties with your hands and place them on a baking sheet lined with baking paper.
5. Brush the meatballs with extra virgin olive oil and season with salt and pepper to taste.
6. Transfer the baking sheet to the basket of the air fryer oven and bake at 180°C for about 20-25 minutes, turning the meatballs halfway through baking to brown them evenly.
7. Serve the chickpea and sweet potato meatballs hot as an appetizer or side dish.

Nutrition per portion: Calories: 350 kcal - Protein: 12 g - Fat: 8 g - Carbohydrates: 58 g - Fiber: 12 g -Sugars: 9 g

Prevent sticking: To prevent the meatballs from sticking to the baking sheet or air fryer basket, you can lightly grease the baking paper with cooking spray or a thin layer of oil. This will ensure that the meatballs retain their shape and don't tear apart when you try to remove them.

Uniform size: Try to make the meatballs as uniform in size as possible to ensure even cooking. Using a cookie scoop or measuring spoon can help you portion out the mixture evenly, resulting in meatballs that cook at the same rate. This way, you'll have perfectly cooked meatballs that are moist on the inside and crispy on the outside.

73. VEGETARIAN CHILI WITH BEANS AND CORN

Prep + Cook time: 40 min | **Serving:** 4 People

Ingredients:

» 2 cups cooked black beans
» 1 cup of corn
» 1 chopped onion
» 2 cloves of garlic, minced
» 2 chopped sweet peppers
» 2 cups peeled tomatoes

» 1 cup vegetable broth
» 1 tablespoon extra virgin olive oil
» 1 tablespoon smoked paprika
» 1 teaspoon cumin
» Salt and pepper to taste

Preparation:

1. Turn on the air fryer oven to 180°C (350°F).
2. In a nonstick skillet, sauté onion, garlic, and bell bell pepper in extra virgin olive oil for about 5-7 minutes until soft.
3. Add the peeled tomatoes, vegetable broth, smoked paprika, and cumin to the pan. Stir well and bring to a boil.
4. Add the black beans and corn to the pan and stir well. Reduce the heat and let it cook for about 15-20 minutes until the chili is thick and the flavors have blended.
5. Transfer the vegetarian chili to the basket of the air fryer oven and bake at 180°C for about 10-15 minutes until it is hot and golden brown on the surface.
6. Serve the vegetarian chili with beans and corn hot as a main dish or side dish.

Nutrition per portion: Calories: 250 kcal - Protein: 10 g - Fat: 6 g - Carbohydrates: 40 g Fiber: 12 g -Sugars: 8 g

Customize the spice level: Adjust the amount of smoked paprika and cumin according to your preference for spiciness. If you prefer a milder chili, reduce the amount of smoked paprika and cum-in. Conversely, if you enjoy a spicier chili, increase the quantities of these spices or add a pinch of cayenne pepper for extra heat.

Enhance the flavor with herbs: Consider adding fresh herbs like cilantro or parsley to your chili for an extra burst of flavor. Stir in a handful of chopped herbs just before serving to add freshness and vibrancy to the dish. You can also garnish each serving with a sprinkle of fresh herbs for a beautiful presentation.

74. VEGETARIAN LASAGNA WITH SPINACH AND RICOTTA CHEESE

Prep + Cook time: 1 hour | **Serving:** 4 People

Ingredients:

- » 1 package of dried lasagna
- » 1 package of fresh spinach
- » 1 cup ricotta cheese
- » 2 cups tomato sauce
- » 1/2 onion, chopped

- » 2 cloves of garlic, minced
- » 1 cup grated mozzarella cheese
- » 1/4 cup grated Parmesan cheese
- » 1 tablespoon of extra virgin olive oil
- » Salt and pepper to taste

Preparation:

1. Turn on the air fryer oven to 180°C (350°F).
2. In a nonstick skillet, sauté onion and garlic in extra virgin olive oil for about 2-3 minutes until golden brown.
3. Add fresh spinach to the pan and cook for about 5-7 minutes until wilted. Drain excess water and let cool.
4. In a bowl, combine the cooled spinach and ricotta cheese. Mix well and adjust salt and pepper to taste.
5. In a pot, cook the dry lasagna in salted boiling water for about 8-10 minutes until al dente. Drain the lasagna and allow it to cool.
6. In an ovenproof baking dish, spread a layer of tomato sauce on the bottom.
7. Arrange a layer of lasagna on top of the tomato sauce.
8. Spread a layer of spinach-ricotta mixture over the lasagna.
9. Add a layer of tomato sauce on top of the spinach-ricotta mixture.
10. Continue arranging layers of lasagna, spinach and ricotta mixture, and tomato sauce until ingredients are exhausted, ending with a layer of tomato sauce.
11. Sprinkle-grated mozzarella and grated Parmigiano Reggiano over the top layer of tomato sauce.
12. Cover the pan with aluminum foil and bake in the air fryer oven at 180°C for about 20-25 minutes.
13. Remove the aluminum foil and bake for another 5-7 minutes until the cheese is golden brown and crispy on the surface.
14. Remove the pan from the air fryer oven and let rest for 5-10 minutes before serving.
15. Serve the vegetarian lasagna hot as a main dish or side dish, accompanied by mixed salad or grilled vegetables to taste.

Nutrition per portion: Calories: 700 kcal - Protein: 36 g - Fat: 26 g - Carbohydrates: 108 g - Fiber: 8 g -Sugars: 10 g

Layer the lasagna evenly: When layering the lasagna, ensure that each layer is spread evenly to create a balanced distribution of flavors and ingredients throughout the dish. This will prevent any one layer from overpowering the others and result in a well-balanced lasagna with every bite.

Let it rest before serving: Allow the lasagna to rest for 5-10 minutes after removing it from the air fryer oven before serving. This allows the lasagna to set and makes it easier to slice into neat portions. Additionally, resting allows the flavors to meld together, resulting in a more flavorful and cohesive dish.

75. QUINOA AND LENTIL BURGER

Prep + Cook time: 1 hour | **Serving:** 4 People

Ingredients:

»   1 cup of quinoa
»   1 cup dried red lentils
»   1 chopped onion
»   3 cloves of garlic, minced
»   2 tablespoons of chickpea flour

»   2 tablespoons extra virgin olive oil
»   1 teaspoon smoked paprika
»   1 teaspoon cumin
»   Salt and pepper to taste

Preparation:

1. Turn on the air fryer oven to 180°C (350°F).
2. In a pot, cook quinoa in salted boiling water for about 15-20 minutes until soft. Drain excess water and allow it to cool.
3. In a separate pot, cook red lentils in salted boiling water for about 15-20 minutes until soft. Drain excess water and allow it to cool.
4. In a nonstick skillet, sauté onion and garlic in extra virgin olive oil for about 2-3 minutes until golden brown.
5. In a large bowl, combine the quinoa, lentils, browned onion and garlic, chickpea flour, smoked paprika, cumin, salt, and pepper. Mix well and lightly mash the lentils with a fork to create an even texture.
6. Form eight uniform burgers with the quinoa and lentil mixture.
7. Transfer the burgers to the basket of an air fryer oven and bake at 180°C (350°F) for about 20-25 minutes, turning them halfway through cooking, until they are golden brown and crisp on the surface.
8. Serve the quinoa and lentil burgers warm with whole wheat bread, salad, and sliced tomatoes as a main dish.

Nutrition per portion: Calories: 322 kcal - Protein: 16 g - Fat: 9 g - Carbohydrates: 46 g - Fiber: 13 g -Sugars: 3 g

Ensure proper texture: After combining all the ingredients, pay attention to the texture of the mixture. It should hold together well when forming the burgers, but not be overly wet or dry. If the mixture feels too wet, you can add a bit more chickpea flour to bind it together. If it feels too dry, you can add a splash of water or vegetable broth to moisten it slightly.

76. PORCINI MUSHROOM RISOTTO

Prep + Cook time: 45 min | **Serving:** 4 People

Ingredients:

- » 1 cup of risotto rice
- » 4 cups vegetable broth
- » 1 chopped onion
- » 2 cloves of garlic, minced
- » 1 cup dried porcini mushrooms

- » 1/2 cup of dry white wine
- » 1/2 cup grated Parmesan cheese
- » 3 tablespoons butter
- » 2 tablespoons of extra virgin olive oil
- » Salt and pepper to taste

Preparation:

1. Turn on the air fryer oven to 180°C (350°F).
2. In a bowl, cover the dried porcini mushrooms with hot water and soak for about 20 minutes until soft. Drain the water and cut the mushrooms into slices. Save the soaking water from the mushrooms.
3. In a nonstick skillet, sauté the onion and garlic in extra virgin olive oil for about 2-3 minutes until golden brown.
4. Add the chopped porcini mushrooms to the pan and cook for about 5-7 minutes until they are soft. Add the risotto rice and toast for about 2-3 minutes until transparent.
5. Add the dry white wine to the pan and stir until the rice absorbs the wine.
6. Gradually add the vegetable broth to the pan, about 1/2 cup at a time, stirring constantly until the rice absorbs the broth.
7. Continue adding the vegetable broth and stirring until the rice is cooked al dente and creamy, about 20-25 minutes.
8. Add the grated Parmesan cheese and butter to the pan and stir until the cheese and butter are melted and the risotto is creamy. Adjust salt and pepper to taste.
9. Transfer the porcini mushroom risotto to an ovenproof dish and bake in the air fryer oven at 180°C (350°F) for about 5-7 minutes until the surface is golden brown and crispy.
10. Serve the porcini mushroom risotto hot as a main dish or side dish, garnished with slices of fresh porcini mushrooms and chopped parsley.

Nutrition per portion: Calories: 425 kcal - Protein: 11 g - Fat: 19 g - Carbohydrates: 47 g - Fiber: 2 g -Sugars: 3 g

77. SAVORY PIE WITH ZUCCHINI AND CARROTS

Prep + Cook time: 45 min | **Serving:** 4-6 People

Ingredients:

» 1 roll of puff pastry
» 2 zucchini cut into thin rounds
» 2 carrots cut into thin rounds
» 1 chopped onion
» 3 eggs

» 1/2 cup of milk
» 1/2 cup grated cheese (such as Parmesan or pecorino)
» 2 tablespoons of extra virgin olive oil
» Salt and pepper to taste

Preparation:

1. Turn on the air fryer oven to 180°C (350°F).
2. In a nonstick skillet, sauté onion in extra virgin olive oil for about 2-3 minutes until golden brown.
3. Add the zucchini and carrots to the pan and cook for about 5-7 minutes until soft. Season with salt and pepper to taste.
4. In a bowl, beat the eggs and add the milk and grated cheese. Mix well.
5. Unroll the puff pastry and place it in a pie pan. Prick the base with a fork.
6. Pour the vegetables into the pan with the puff pastry and spread them evenly.
7. Pour the egg, milk, and cheese mixture over the vegetables.
8. Transfer the pan to the basket of the air fryer oven and bake at 180°C (350°F) for about 25-30 minutes until the savory pie is golden brown on the surface and the eggs are cooked.
9. Serve the savory cake with zucchini and carrots warm as an appetizer or main course.

Nutrition per portion: Calories: 709 kcal - Protein: 12 g - Fat: 52 g - Carbohydrates: 59 g - Fiber: 3 g -Sugars: 5 g

Precook the puff pastry: Before adding the vegetables and egg mixture, consider pre-baking the puff pastry for a few minutes in the air fryer oven. This will help ensure that the bottom of the pie crust cooks evenly and remains crispy, preventing it from becoming soggy from the moisture released by the vegetables and egg mixture.

Layer the vegetables evenly: When spreading the cooked zucchini and carrots onto the puff pastry, ensure that they are distributed evenly across the surface. This will help ensure that each bite of the pie contains a balanced mixture of vegetables and flavors. Additionally, evenly layering the vegetables will help the pie cook more evenly and result in a visually appealing presentation.

SANDWICHES AND PIZZA RECIPES

78. HAM AND MOZZARELLA CHEESE SANDWICH

Prep: 10 minutes | **Cook time:** 5-7 minutes | **Serving:** 2 sandwiches

Ingredients:

- » 2 ciabatta sandwiches
- » 4 slices of prosciutto
- » 4 slices of mozzarella cheese
- » 4 lettuce leaves
- » 1 sliced tomato
- » 2 tablespoons mayonnaise
- » 1 teaspoon mustard
- » Salt and pepper to taste

Preparation:

1. Turn on the air fryer oven to 180°C (350°F).
2. Cut the ciabatta buns in half and toast them lightly in the air fryer oven.
3. In a bowl, mix mayonnaise and mustard until smooth.
4. Spread the creamy mayonnaise-mustard mixture on the ciabatta buns.
5. Add the ham slices, mozzarella slices, lettuce leaves, and tomato slices to the sandwiches.
6. Season with salt and pepper to taste.
7. Close the sandwiches and transfer them to the basket of the air fryer oven.
8. Bake the sandwiches at 180°C for about 5-7 minutes until the mozzarella cheese is melted and the bread is crispy on the surface.
9. Serve the ham and mozzarella sandwiches hot as a main dish or quick snack.

Nutrition per portion: Calories: 550 kcal | Protein: 28g | Fats: 27g | Carbohydrates: 50 g - Fiber: 3 g -Sugars: 3.5 g

Layer the ingredients evenly: When assembling the sandwiches, make sure to distribute the ingredients evenly between the two sandwiches. This ensures that each bite contains a balanced combination of flavors. Layer the prosciutto, mozzarella, lettuce, and tomato neatly on the ciabatta buns to create a visually appealing and satisfying sandwich.

79. TUNA AND SUN-DRIED TOMATO SANDWICH

Prep: 10 minutes | **Cook time:** 5-7 minutes | **Serving:** 2 sandwiches

Ingredients:

- » 2 olive sandwiches
- » 1 can of natural tuna
- » 4 sun-dried tomatoes in oil
- » 2 tablespoons mayonnaise

- » 1 teaspoon mustard
- » 1/2 lemon (just the juice)
- » 1/4 thinly sliced red onion
- » Salt and pepper to taste

Preparation:

1. Turn on the air fryer oven to 180°C (350°F).
2. Cut the olive rolls in half and toast them lightly in the air fryer oven.
3. In a bowl, drain the natural tuna and mash it with a fork.
4. Add the chopped dried tomatoes in oil to the tuna bowl and mix well.
5. In a separate bowl, mix the mayonnaise, mustard, and lemon juice until smooth.
6. Spread the cream of mayonnaise and mustard on the olive sandwiches.
7. Add the tuna and sun-dried tomatoes to the sandwiches.
8. Add the red onion slices to the sandwiches.
9. Season with salt and pepper to taste.
10. Close the buns and transfer them to the basket of the air fryer oven.
11. Bake the sandwiches at 180°C for about 5-7 minutes until the bread is crispy on the surface.
12. Serve the sandwiches with tuna and sun-dried tomatoes hot as a main dish or quick snack.

Nutrition per portion: Calories: 430 kcal | Protein: 25g | Fats: 20g | Carbohydrates: 35g - Fiber: 7 g -Sugars: 10 g

Drain excess oil from the sun-dried tomatoes: Before adding the sun-dried tomatoes to the tuna mixture, pat them dry with a paper towel to remove any excess oil. This prevents the sandwiches from becoming too oily and ensures a better texture and flavor balance in each bite.

Prevent soggy bread: To prevent the bread from becoming soggy spread a thin layer of mayonnaise or mustard on the inside of each bread slice before adding the tuna mixture. This creates a barrier between the filling and the bread, helping to maintain the bread's texture and preventing it from getting mushy, especially if you're making the sandwiches ahead of time.

80. CHICKEN AND AVOCADO SANDWICH

Prep: 10 minutes | **Cook time:** 5-7 minutes | **Serving:** 2 sandwiches

Ingredients:

- » 2 cereal sandwiches
- » 2 cooked and sliced chicken breasts
- » 1 sliced ripe avocado
- » 2 lettuce leaves
- » 2 slices of tomato

- » 2 tablespoons mayonnaise
- » 1 teaspoon mustard
- » Juice of half a lemon
- » Salt and pepper to taste

Preparation:

1. Turn on the air fryer oven to 180°C (350°F).
2. Cut the cereal rolls in half and toast them lightly in the air fryer oven.
3. In a bowl, mix mayonnaise, mustard, and lemon juice until smooth.
4. Spread the creamy mayonnaise-mustard mixture on the cereal sandwiches.
5. Add the chicken slices, avocado slices, lettuce leaves, and tomato slices to the sandwiches.
6. Adjust salt and pepper to taste.
7. Close the sandwiches and transfer them to the basket of the air fryer oven.
8. Bake the sandwiches at 180°C for about 5-7 minutes until the bread is crispy on the surface.
9. Serve the chicken and avocado sandwiches hot as a main dish or quick snack.

Nutrition per portion: Calories: 470 kcal | Protein: 28g | Fats: 22g | Carbohydrates: 32g - Fiber: 20 g -Sugars: 8 g

Enhance the flavor with seasoning: Consider seasoning the chicken breasts with your favorite spices or herbs before cooking them. This adds extra flavor to the chicken and elevates the taste of the sandwiches. Options like garlic powder, smoked paprika, or Italian seasoning can complement the creamy avocado and add depth to the overall flavor profile.

Add a tangy twist: For a burst of freshness and tanginess, consider adding thinly sliced red onion or pickles to the sandwiches. The sharpness of the onion or the tanginess of the pickles can contrast nicely with the creamy avocado and savory chicken, adding complexity to each bite. Adjust the amount according to your preference to balance the flavors.

81. FOCACCIA WITH CHERRY TOMATOES AND BASIL

Prep: 5 minutes | **Cook time:** 10-12 minutes | **Serving:** 1 focaccia

Ingredients:

» 1 focaccia
» 10 halved cherry tomatoes
» 1/2 cup fresh basil

» 2 tablespoons extra virgin olive oil
» 1 clove of garlic, minced
» Salt and pepper to taste

Preparation:

1. Turn on the air fryer oven to 180°C (350°F).
2. Cut the focaccia in half and place it in the basket of the air fryer oven.
3. In a bowl, mix the extra virgin olive oil and minced garlic.
4. Spread the oil and garlic mixture on the focaccia.
5. Add the halved cherry tomatoes to the focaccia.
6. Season with salt and pepper to taste.
7. Bake the focaccia at 180°C (350°F) for about 10-12 minutes until the bread is golden brown and crisp on the surface.
8. Remove the focaccia from the air fryer oven and add fresh basil on top of the focaccia.
9. Serve the focaccia with cherry tomatoes and basil warm as an appetizer or accompaniment to a dinner party.

Nutrition per portion: Calories: 350-400 kcal | Protein: 5-7g | Fats: 15-20g | Carbohydrates: 45-50g - Fiber: 20 g -Sugars: 8 g

Infuse the olive oil with herbs: Take your focaccia to the next level by infusing the extra virgin olive oil with herbs before spreading it on the bread. Simply heat the olive oil in a small saucepan over low heat with fresh herbs like rosemary, thyme, or oregano. Let it simmer for a few minutes to infuse the oil with the herbs' flavors, then strain out the herbs and mix the garlic into the infused oil before spreading it on the focaccia. This adds an extra layer of aromatic flavor to your dish.

Experiment with cheese: Consider adding a sprinkle of grated Parmesan or crumbled feta cheese over the cherry tomatoes before baking the focaccia. The cheese will melt and become golden and crispy during baking, adding a savory dimension to the dish. Alternatively, you can also incorporate slices of fresh mozzarella cheese between the cherry tomatoes for a gooey and indulgent touch. Adjust the amount of cheese according to your taste preferences for a deliciously cheesy focaccia experience.

82. PIZZA MARGHERITA

Prep: 5 minutes | **Cook time:** 10-12 minutes | **Serving:** 1 pizza

Ingredients:

» 1 pizza base
» 1/2 cup tomato sauce
» 1 cup of grated mozzarella cheese

» 1/4 cup grated Parmesan cheese
» Fresh basil leaves
» Salt and pepper to taste

Preparation:

1. Turn on the air fryer oven to 180°C (350°F).
2. Place the pizza base on the basket of the air fryer oven.
3. Spread tomato sauce on the pizza base.
4. Add grated mozzarella cheese on top of the tomato sauce.
5. Season with salt and pepper to taste.
6. Bake the pizza at 180°C for about 10-12 minutes until the cheese is melted and the edge of the pizza is golden and crispy on the surface.
7. Remove the pizza from the air fryer oven and add grated Parmesan cheese and fresh basil leaves on top of the pizza.
8. Serve the pizza Margherita hot as a main dish or side dish, accompanied by mixed salad or grilled vegetables to taste. Enjoy!

Nutrition per portion: Calories: 500-550 kcal | Protein: 20-25g | Fats: 25-30g | Carbohydrates: 30-35g - Fiber: 2 g -Sugars: 2 g

Upgrade your tomato sauce: Elevate the flavor of your Pizza Margherita by preparing a homemade tomato sauce with fresh ingredients. Sauté minced garlic and diced onions in olive oil until softened, then add crushed tomatoes, a pinch of sugar, and a sprinkle of dried oregano and basil. Simmer the sauce for about 15-20 minutes until it thickens, then spread it onto your pizza base. This homemade sauce will impart a rich and savory flavor to your pizza, enhancing its overall taste.

Experiment with toppings: While the classic Pizza Margherita traditionally consists of tomato sauce, mozzarella cheese, and fresh basil, feel free to get creative with additional toppings. Consider adding sliced cherry tomatoes or roasted red peppers for extra sweetness and a burst of color. You can also incorporate toppings like thinly sliced onions, olives, or mushrooms for added flavor and texture. Customize your Pizza Margherita to suit your taste preferences and make it truly unique.

83. EGGPLANT AND GOAT CHEESE SANDWICH

Prep: 15 minutes | **Cook time:** 10-12 minutes | **Serving:** 2 sandwiches

Ingredients:

- » 2 whole wheat bread sandwiches
- » 1 sliced eggplant
- » 4 slices of goat cheese
- » 2 tablespoons mayonnaise
- » 1/2 lemon (just the juice)
- » 1 clove of garlic, minced
- » 1 tablespoon extra virgin olive oil
- » Salt and pepper to taste

Preparation:

1. Turn on the air fryer oven to 180°C (350°F).
2. Cut whole wheat bread rolls in half and toast them lightly in the air fryer oven.
3. In a bowl, mix mayonnaise and lemon juice until smooth.
4. Spread the creamy mayonnaise on the whole wheat bread sandwiches.
5. In a nonstick skillet, grill eggplant slices with extra virgin olive oil and minced garlic for about 4-5 minutes per side until soft and lightly browned.
6. Season with salt and pepper to taste.
7. Add the slices of goat cheese over the eggplant slices and melt them slightly.
8. Add the eggplant and goat cheese slices to the sandwiches.
9. Close the sandwiches and transfer them to the basket of the air fryer oven.
10. Bake the sandwiches at 180°C for about 5-7 minutes until the bread is crispy on the surface.
11. Serve the sandwiches with grilled eggplant and goat cheese hot as a main dish or a quick snack.

Nutrition per portion: 400-450 kcal | Protein: 15-20g | Fats: 20-25g | Carbohydrates: 35-40g - Fiber: 5 g -Sugars: 5 g

Marinate the eggplant: Before grilling the eggplant, consider marinating it to infuse it with extra flavor. Create a marinade using a mixture of extra virgin olive oil, balsamic vinegar, minced garlic, dried oregano, and a pinch of red pepper flakes for some heat. Coat the eggplant slices in the marinade and let them sit for at least 15-20 minutes before grilling. This will not only add depth of flavor to the eggplant but also help tenderize it, resulting in a more succulent and flavorful sandwich.

84. PIZZA WITH MUSHROOMS AND SAUSAGE

Prep + Cook time: 15-20 min

Ingredients:

»   1 pizza base
»   1 cup sliced fresh mushrooms
»   1/2 cup crumbled sausage
»   1 cup grated mozzarella cheese

»   1/4 cup tomato sauce
»   1 tablespoon extra virgin olive oil
»   1 clove of garlic, minced
»   Salt and pepper to taste

Preparation:

1. Preheat the oven to 220°C.
2. In a skillet, heat extra virgin olive oil and minced garlic for 1-2 minutes.
3. Add the mushrooms and crumbled sausage and cook for 5-7 minutes, until the mushrooms are soft.
4. Spread the pizza base on a pizza pan and spread the tomato sauce on top.
5. Spread the grated mozzarella cheese evenly over the tomato sauce.
6. Add the mushroom and sausage mixture over the mozzarella cheese.
7. Bake the pizza for 12-15 minutes, until the cheese is melted and the edge of the pizza is golden brown.
8. Remove pizza from oven, cut into slices, and serve hot.

Nutrition per portion: Calories: 360-400 kcal, Protein: 20-25g, Fats: 20-25g, Carbohydrates: 25-30g - Fibre: 2-3g - Zuccheri: 2-3g

Layer the ingredients: To ensure an even distribution of toppings and flavors, consider layering the ingredients strategically. Start with the tomato sauce as the base, followed by a layer of grated mozzarella cheese. Then, add the cooked mushroom and sausage mixture on top. This layering technique will help prevent the toppings from sliding off the pizza while baking and ensure that each bite is packed with delicious flavors.

Add fresh herbs: Elevate the taste of your pizza by adding fresh herbs before or after baking. Consider sprinkling some chopped fresh basil or oregano over the pizza just before serving. The aromatic herbs will complement the savory flavors of the mushrooms and sausage, adding brightness and freshness to each slice. Alternatively, you can also drizzle a bit of extra virgin olive oil infused with herbs over the pizza after baking for an extra burst of flavor.

85. CALZONE WITH HAM AND CHEESE

Ingredients:

» 1 pizza base
» 4 slices of cooked ham
» 1 cup grated mozzarella cheese
» 1/2 cup tomato sauce
» 1 clove of minced garlic
» 1 tablespoon extra virgin olive oil
» Salt and pepper to taste

Preparation:

1. Preheat the oven to 220°C.
2. In a skillet, heat extra virgin olive oil and minced garlic for 1-2 minutes.
3. Add the tomato sauce and cook for 5-7 minutes, until the sauce has thickened slightly.
4. Spread the pizza base on a pizza pan and spread the tomato sauce on half of the base.
5. Spread the grated mozzarella cheese evenly over the tomato sauce.
6. Add the prosciutto slices on top of the mozzarella cheese.
7. Fold the other half of the pizza base over the filling and seal the edges of the calzone tightly.
8. Bake the calzone for 12 to 15 minutes, until the crust is golden brown and crispy.
9. Remove the calzone from the oven, cut it in half, and serve hot.

Nutrition per portion: Calories: 500-550 kcal, Protein: 25-30g, Fats: 25-30g, Carbohydrates: 30-35g - Fibre: 2-3g - Zuccheri: 2-3g

Add fresh herbs: Incorporate fresh herbs like basil or oregano into the tomato sauce for added flavor. Simply chop the herbs finely and mix them into the sauce before spreading it onto the pizza base. The herbs will infuse the sauce with aromatic notes and elevate the overall taste of the calzone.

Experiment with cheese: While mozzarella cheese is a classic choice for calzones, you can experiment with different types of cheese to customize the flavor profile. Try adding a sprinkle of grated Parmesan or Pecorino Romano cheese along with the mozzarella for a more complex and savory taste. Alternatively, you can use a blend of cheeses like provolone, fontina, or gouda to create a rich and gooey cheese filling for your calzone.

86. SALMON AND ARUGULA PIZZA

Prep: 10 minutes | **Cook time:** 12-15 minutes | **Serving:** 1

Ingredients:

» 1 pizza base
» 1/2 cup tomato sauce
» 1 cup grated mozzarella cheese
» 4-6 slices of smoked salmon
» 1/2 cup arugula
» 1 tablespoon extra virgin olive oil
» Salt and pepper to taste

Preparation:

1. Preheat the oven to 220°C (350°F).
2. Spread the pizza base on a pizza pan and spread tomato sauce on top.
3. Spread the grated mozzarella cheese evenly over the tomato sauce.
4. Arrange the salmon slices on top of the mozzarella cheese.
5. Bake the pizza for about 12 to 15 minutes, until the cheese is melted and the edge of the pizza is golden brown.
6. Remove the pizza from the oven and add the arugula on top.
7. Drizzle with extra virgin olive oil, salt, and pepper to taste.
8. Cut the pizza into slices and serve hot.

Nutrition per portion: Calories: 350-400 kcal, Protein: 20-25g, Fats: 15-20g, Carbohydrates: 30-35g - Fiber: 2-3g – Sugars: 2-3g

Citrus zest: Before baking the pizza, consider grating some lemon or lime zest over the top. The zest will infuse the pizza with bright citrus flavors that complement the richness of the smoked salmon and the peppery arugula. Simply sprinkle the zest evenly over the pizza after adding the salmon slices and before baking.

Creamy sauce drizzle: Create a creamy and tangy sauce to drizzle over the finished pizza for added flavor and richness. Mix together equal parts of Greek yogurt and sour cream, then add a splash of lemon juice and a pinch of salt. Stir until smooth and creamy. After removing the pizza from the oven, drizzle the creamy sauce over the top, focusing on the areas with the smoked salmon and arugula. This sauce will add a delightful contrast to the other flavors and textures on the pizza.

87. SANDWICH WITH MEATBALLS AND TOMATO SAUCE

Prep: 20 minutes | **Cook time:** 12-15 minutes | **Serving:** 2

Ingredients:

» 2 soft sandwiches
» 6 meatballs
» 1/2 cup of tomato sauce
» 4 slices of cheese
» Spray oil for air fryer
» For the meatballs:
» 500 g ground meat (beef or mixed)

» 1 egg
» 1/2 cup breadcrumbs
» 1/4 cup milk
» 1/4 cup grated cheese (parmesan or pecorino)
» 1/4 cup chopped fresh parsley
» 1/2 teaspoon of garlic powder
» Salt and pepper to taste

Preparation:

1. In a bowl, combine the ground meat, egg, bread crumbs, milk, grated cheese, parsley, garlic powder, salt and pepper. Mix well until the mixture is smooth.
2. Take a portion of the meat mixture and form a patty with your hands, the desired size. Repeat the process until the mixture is used up.
3. Preheat the Breville Pro air fryer to 200°C.
4. Place the meatballs on the air fryer grill and spray them with spray oil.
5. Cook the meatballs for about 12 to 15 minutes, turning them halfway through cooking, until they are cooked through and golden brown.
6. Cut the sandwiches in half and stuff each sandwich with 3 meatballs and 2 slices of cheese.
7. Add the tomato sauce to the stuffed sandwiches with the meatballs and cheese.
8. Close the sandwiches tightly and place them on the grill of the Breville Pro air fryer.
9. Cook the sandwiches for about 2-3 minutes, until the cheese is melted and the sandwich is golden brown.
10. Remove the sandwiches from the air fryer and serve hot.

Nutrition per portion: Calories: 500-550 kcal, Protein: 30-35g, Fats: 25-30g, Carbohydrates: 30-35g - Fiber: 3-4g - Sugars: 4-6g

DESSERT RECIPES

88. AIR FRYER OVEN STRAWBERRY TIRAMISU

Prep: 30 minutes | **Cook time:** 5-7 minutes | **Serving:** 8-10

Ingredients:

» 1 lb fresh strawberries, washed, hulled, and sliced
» 1 cup heavy cream
» 1/2 cup powdered sugar
» 1 cup mascarpone cheese
» 1 tsp vanilla extract
» 1 cup strong brewed coffee, cooled to room temperature
» 2 tbsp coffee liqueur (optional)
» 24 ladyfinger cookies
» Cocoa powder or grated chocolate for dusting
» Fresh mint leaves for garnish (optional)

Instructions:

1. In a mixing bowl, whip the heavy cream with an electric mixer until soft peaks form. Gradually add the powdered sugar and continue to whip until stiff peaks form.
2. In another bowl, mix the mascarpone cheese and vanilla extract until well combined. Gently fold the whipped cream into the mascarpone mixture until smooth and creamy.
3. In a shallow dish, combine the brewed coffee and coffee liqueur (if using).
4. Dip each ladyfinger into the coffee mixture, ensuring they are soaked but not overly soggy. Line the bottom of your air fryer oven's baking dish with a layer of soaked ladyfingers.
5. Spoon half of the mascarpone and whipped cream mixture over the ladyfingers, spreading it evenly.
6. Add a layer of sliced strawberries on top of the cream mixture.
7. Repeat the process with another layer of soaked ladyfingers, followed by the remaining cream mixture, and finally, another layer of sliced strawberries.
8. Cover the baking dish with plastic wrap and refrigerate the tiramisu for at least 4 hours or preferably overnight to allow the flavors to meld together.
9. Preheat your air fryer oven to 350°F (175°C).
10. Once the tiramisu has chilled and set, remove the plastic wrap and place the baking dish in the air fryer basket.
11. Air fry the tiramisu for about 5-7 minutes until the top becomes slightly golden and the edges are crispy.
12. Remove the tiramisu from the air fryer and let it cool for a few minutes.
13. Before serving, dust the top of the tiramisu with cocoa powder or grated chocolate.
14. Garnish with fresh mint leaves if desired.
15. Slice and serve the delicious Air Fryer Oven Strawberry Tiramisu, and enjoy!

Nutrition per portion: 317 kcal - Protein: 5g - Fat: 23g - Carbohydrates: 24g - Fiber: 2g - Sugars: 12g

89. AIR FRYER OVEN CHOCOLATE CHEESECAKE

Prep: 20 min | **Cook time:** 30 min | **Serving:** 6-8 slices

Ingredients:

- 1 1/2 cups graham cracker crumbs
- 1/4 cup granulated sugar
- 1/2 cup unsalted butter, melted
- 2 cups cream cheese, softened
- 1/2 cup sour cream
- 1/2 cup granulated sugar

- 2 large eggs
- 1 teaspoon vanilla extract
- 1/2 cup semisweet chocolate chips, melted
- Optional toppings: chocolate syrup, whipped cream, chocolate shavings

Instructions:

1. Preheat your air fryer oven to 320°F (160°C).
2. In a medium bowl, mix the graham cracker crumbs, 1/4 cup sugar, and melted butter until well combined. Press the mixture into the bottom of a 7-inch springform pan to form the crust.
3. In a large mixing bowl, beat the softened cream cheese, sour cream, and 1/2 cup sugar until smooth and creamy.
4. Add the eggs one at a time, beating well after each addition. Stir in the vanilla extract.
5. Melt the chocolate chips in a microwave-safe bowl, stirring every 15 seconds until smooth. Let it cool slightly, then add it to the cream cheese mixture, and mix until well combined.
6. Pour the cream cheese mixture over the gra-ham cracker crust in the springform pan.
7. Place the pan into the air fryer oven and cook at 320°F (160°C) for about 30 minutes or until the edges are set, and the center is slightly jiggly.
8. Turn off the air fryer oven and leave the cheesecake inside with the door slightly ajar for about 15-20 minutes.
9. Remove the cheesecake from the air fryer oven and let it cool to room temperature. Once cooled, refrigerate it for at least 2 hours or overnight to set.
10. When serving, you can add optional toppings like chocolate syrup, whipped cream, or chocolate shavings.

Nutrition: Calories: 420 kcal Total Fat: 29g Total Carbohydrates: 34g Sugars: 24g Protein: 6g

90. AIR FRYER LEMON DOUGHNUT

Prep: 15 min | **Cook time:** 8 min | **Serving:** 8 doughnuts

Ingredients:

- » 1 cup all-purpose flour
- » 1/3 cup granulated sugar
- » 1 teaspoon baking powder
- » 1/4 teaspoon baking soda
- » 1/4 teaspoon salt
- » 1/3 cup buttermilk
- » 1 large egg
- » 2 tablespoons unsalted butter, melted

- » 1 tablespoon lemon zest
- » 1 tablespoon fresh lemon juice
- » 1/2 teaspoon vanilla extract
- » For the Glaze:
- » 1/2 cup powdered sugar
- » 1 tablespoon fresh lemon juice
- » 1/2 teaspoon lemon zest

Instructions:

1. Preheat your air fryer oven to 350°F (175°C) for 5 minutes.
2. In a large mixing bowl, whisk together the flour, granulated sugar, baking powder, baking soda, and salt.
3. In a separate bowl, mix the buttermilk, egg, melted butter, lemon zest, lemon juice, and vanilla extract until well combined.
4. Gradually pour the wet ingredients into the dry ingredients, stirring until just combined. Be careful not to overmix; a few lumps are okay.
5. Lightly grease the air fryer basket or use parchment paper rounds to prevent sticking. Spoon the doughnut batter into a piping bag or a plastic ziplock bag with the corner snipped off.
6. Pipe the batter into the doughnut molds in the air fryer basket, filling each cavity about 2/3

full.
7. Air fry the doughnuts at 350°F (175°C) for 8 minutes or until they are golden brown and cooked through. You may need to do this in batches depending on the size of your air fryer.
8. While the doughnuts are cooking, prepare the glaze by whisking together powdered sugar, lemon juice, and lemon zest in a small bowl until smooth.
9. Once the doughnuts are done, remove them from the air fryer and let them cool for a few minutes.
10. Dip each doughnut into the glaze, allowing the excess glaze to drip off. Place them on a wire rack to set.
11. Serve the lemon doughnuts warm or at room temperature.

Nutrition per portion: Calories: 180 kcal - Protein: 3g - Fat: 4g - Carbohydrates: 34g - Fiber: 1-2 g - Sugars: 17g

91. AIR FRYER OVEN DARK CHOCOLATE BROWNIES

Prep: 15 min | **Cook time:** 20-25 min | **Serving:** 9-12 brownies

Ingredients:

- » 1/2 cup unsalted butter, melted
- » 1 cup granulated sugar
- » 2 large eggs
- » 1 teaspoon vanilla extract
- » 1/2 cup all-purpose flour
- » 1/3 cup unsweetened cocoa powder
- » 1/4 teaspoon baking powder
- » 1/4 teaspoon salt
- » 1/2 cup dark chocolate chips
- » Optional Add-ins (nuts, etc.):
- » 1/2 cup chopped walnuts or pecans (optional)

Instructions:

1. Preheat your air fryer oven to 350°F (175°C) for a few minutes.
2. In a large mixing bowl, combine the melted butter and granulated sugar. Mix well until smooth and slightly fluffy.
3. Add the eggs one at a time, mixing well after each addition. Stir in the vanilla extract.
4. In a separate bowl, whisk together the all-purpose flour, unsweetened cocoa powder, baking powder, and salt.
5. Gradually add the dry ingredients to the wet ingredients in the mixing bowl. Stir until just combined, making sure not to overmix.
6. If you're adding nuts, gently fold in the chopped walnuts or pecans at this stage.
7. Grease a baking dish that fits into your air fryer oven and pour the brownie batter into it. Smooth the top with a spatula.
8. Sprinkle the dark chocolate chips evenly over the batter.
9. Place the baking dish in the preheated air fryer oven and cook for 20 to 25 minutes or until a toothpick inserted into the center comes out with a few moist crumbs (avoid overbaking to keep the brownies fudgy).
10. Once done, remove the brownies from the air fryer oven and let them cool in the baking dish for a few minutes before slicing.
11. Serve warm or at room temperature. Optionally, you can dust the brownies with powdered sugar or serve them with a scoop of vanilla ice cream.

Nutrition per portion: Calories: 250 kcal - Total Fat: 14g - Saturated Fat: 8g - Sugars: 20g - Protein: 3g – Fiber: 2 g - Sugars: 20 g -

92. AIR FRYER OVEN BANANA AND CHOCOLATE MUFFINS

Prep: 15 min | **Cook time:** 15 min | **Serving:** 6 muffins

Ingredients:

- » 2 ripe bananas, mashed
- » 1/4 cup vegetable oil
- » 1/3 cup brown sugar
- » 1 large egg
- » 1 teaspoon vanilla extract
- » 1 cup all-purpose flour

- » 1 teaspoon baking powder
- » 1/2 teaspoon baking soda
- » 1/4 teaspoon salt
- » 1/4 cup unsweetened cocoa powder
- » 1/4 cup milk (dairy or plant-based)
- » 1/2 cup semisweet chocolate chips

Instructions:

1. Preheat your air fryer oven to 350°F (175°C) for 5 minutes.
2. In a large mixing bowl, combine the mashed bananas, vegetable oil, brown sugar, egg, and vanilla extract. Mix well.
3. In a separate bowl, whisk together the all-purpose flour, baking powder, baking soda, salt, and unsweetened cocoa powder.
4. Gradually add the dry ingredients to the banana mixture, alternating with the milk. Stir until just combined. Be careful not to overmix.
5. Fold in the semisweet chocolate chips into the batter.
6. Line the air fryer basket or muffin tray with muffin liners. Spoon the muffin batter evenly into the muffin cups, filling each about 2/3 full.
7. Place the muffins in the air fryer oven basket or on the muffin tray, making sure they are not too close together.
8. Air fry the muffins at 350°F (175°C) for approximately 12-15 minutes or until a toothpick inserted in the center comes out clean.
9. Once done, remove the muffins from the air fryer oven and let them cool in the muffin tray for a few minutes before transferring them to a wire rack to cool completely.

Nutrition per portion: Calories: 235 kcal - Carbohydrates: 34 g - Protein: 4 g - Fat: 14 g - Saturated Fat: 2.5 g – Fiber: 2 g – Sugars: 20 g

93. AIR FRYER OVEN CATALAN CREAM WITH CARAMEL

Prep: 15 min | **Cook time:** 40 min | **Serving:** 4-6

Ingredients:

- » 4 large egg yolks
- » 1/4 cup granulated sugar
- » 2 cups whole milk
- » 1 tsp vanilla extract

- » 1 cinnamon stick
- » 1 lemon peel (strips)
- » 4-6 tbsp granulated sugar (for caramelizing)
- » Fresh fruit or mint leaves (for garnish)

Instructions:

1. In a saucepan, heat the milk, cinnamon stick, and lemon peel over medium heat. Bring to a gentle simmer, then remove from heat and let it cool for about 15-20 minutes.
2. In a mixing bowl, whisk together the egg yolks and 1/4 cup of granulated sugar until smooth and creamy.
3. Gradually add the cooled milk mixture to the egg yolk mixture while whisking constantly.
4. Remove the cinnamon stick and lemon peel from the mixture and stir in the vanilla extract.
5. Preheat your air fryer oven to 325°F (160°C).
6. Pour the custard mixture into individual ramekins or oven-safe serving dishes.
7. Place the ramekins in the preheated air fryer oven and cook for about 35-40 minutes or until the edges are set but the center is slightly jiggly.
8. Remove the ramekins from the air fryer oven and let them cool to room temperature. Then refrigerate them for at least 2 hours or until fully chilled.
9. Just before serving, sprinkle 1 tablespoon of granulated sugar evenly over the surface of each custard. Use a kitchen torch to caramelize the sugar until it forms a crispy and golden-brown layer.
10. Garnish with fresh fruit or mint leaves and serve immediately.

Nutrition: Calories: 220-260 kcal, Carbohydrates: 35-40g, Protein: 5-6g, Fat: 6-8g

Use Room-Temperature Ingredients for a Smooth Custard: To ensure a smooth and creamy custard, use room-temperature egg yolks and gradually incorporate the cooled milk mixture. This helps to avoid curdling and ensures a uniform texture. After heating the milk with the cinnamon stick and lemon peel, let it cool sufficiently but make sure it's still slightly warm when adding it to the egg mixture. This gentle heating process tempers the eggs and prevents them from scrambling.

Achieve an Even Caramelized Top: For a perfectly even caramelized top, ensure the granulated sugar is spread in a thin, uniform layer over the custard. When using a kitchen torch, move the torch in a circular motion and keep it at a consistent distance from the surface to avoid burning one spot while other areas remain uncaramelized. If you don't have a kitchen torch, you can caramelize the sugar under the broiler of your air fryer oven, watching closely to prevent burning.

By following these tips, you'll create a smooth, creamy Catalan Cream with a perfectly caramelized top using your Breville Pro air fryer oven. Enjoy your dessert!

94. AIR FRYER OVEN APPLE AND CINNAMON CRUMBLE

Prep: 15 min | **Cook time:** 20 min | **Serving:** 4

Ingredients:

» 4 medium-sized apples (such as Granny Smith or Honeycrisp), peeled, cored, and chopped into small pieces
» 1 tablespoon lemon juice
» 1/4 cup granulated sugar
» 1 teaspoon ground cinnamon
» 1/4 teaspoon ground nutmeg

» 1/2 cup old-fashioned rolled oats
» 1/4 cup all-purpose flour
» 1/4 cup brown sugar (light or dark)
» 3 tablespoons unsalted butter, cold and cut into small pieces
» Optional: Vanilla ice cream or whipped cream for serving

Instructions:

1. Preheat your air fryer oven to 375°F (190°C).
2. In a mixing bowl, combine the chopped apples with lemon juice, granulated sugar, cinnamon, and nutmeg. Toss until the apples are evenly coated.
3. In a separate bowl, mix the rolled oats, all-purpose flour, and brown sugar. Add the cold butter pieces and use your fingers to work the butter into the dry ingredients until the mixture resembles coarse crumbs.
4. Transfer the apple mixture to a baking dish that fits inside your air fryer oven. Spread it out evenly.
5. Sprinkle the oat crumble mixture on top of the apples.
6. Place the baking dish in the air fryer oven and cook at 375°F (190°C) for about 20 minutes or until the apples are tender and the topping is golden brown and crisp.
7. Once done, remove the crumble from the air fryer oven and let it cool slightly.
8. Serve the apple and cinnamon crumble warm, optionally topped with a scoop of vanilla ice cream or a dollop of whipped cream.

Nutrition per portion: Calories: 230-250 kcal Fat: 14 g Carbohydrates: 31 g Protein: 3g – Sugars: 20 g

Ensure Even Cooking by Slicing Apples Uniformly: To achieve even cooking and a consistent texture, make sure to chop the apples into uniform small pieces. This ensures that all the apple pieces cook at the same rate, avoiding some being undercooked while others are overcooked. Using apples like Granny Smith or Honeycrisp, which hold their shape well during cooking, will also help maintain the texture of the crumble.

95. AIR FRYER OVEN CHOCOLATE AND HAZELNUT CAKE

Prep: 15 min | **Cook time:** 30 min | **Serving:** 8

Ingredients:

» 1 cup all-purpose flour
» 1/2 cup cocoa powder
» 1 teaspoon baking powder
» 1/2 teaspoon baking soda
» 1/4 teaspoon salt
» 1/2 cup granulated sugar
» 1/2 cup brown sugar

» 1/2 cup vegetable oil
» 2 large eggs
» 1 teaspoon vanilla extract
» 1/2 cup buttermilk
» 1/2 cup chopped hazelnuts
» Cooking spray (for greasing the air fryer oven pan)

Instructions:

1. Preheat your air fryer oven to 350°F (175°C) for a few minutes.
2. In a large bowl, whisk together the flour, cocoa powder, baking powder, baking soda, and salt.
3. In another bowl, whisk together the granulated sugar, brown sugar, vegetable oil, eggs, and vanilla extract until well combined.
4. Gradually add the dry ingredients to the wet ingredients, alternating with the buttermilk, and mix until just combined. Do not overmix.
5. Fold the chopped hazelnuts into the batter.
6. Grease a round cake pan that fits in your air fryer oven with cooking spray.
7. Pour the cake batter into the prepared cake pan.
8. Place the cake pan in the air fryer oven and cook at 350°F (175°C) for about 25-30 minutes or until a toothpick inserted in the center comes out clean.
9. Once done, remove the cake from the air fryer oven and let it cool in the pan for a few minutes before transferring it to a wire rack to cool completely.

Nutrition per portion: Calories: 290 kcal – Fat: 16 g - Carbohydrates: 31g - Protein: 4 g - Fiber: 2 g - Sugars: 24 g

Prevent Overmixing for a Tender Cake: When combining the wet and dry ingredients, be sure to mix just until they are incorporated. Overmixing the batter can lead to a dense and tough cake because it overdevelops the gluten in the flour.

96. AIR FRYER OVEN HOMEMADE VANILLA ICE CREAM

Prep: 10 min | **Cook time:** 20 min | **Serving:** 4

Ingredients:

» 2 cups heavy cream
» 1 cup whole milk
» 3/4 cup granulated sugar

» 1 tablespoon pure vanilla extract
» Pinch of salt

Instructions:

1. In a medium-sized mixing bowl, whisk together the heavy cream, whole milk, granulated sugar, vanilla extract, and a pinch of salt until the sugar is fully dissolved.
2. Pour the mixture into a shallow, freezer-safe container. You can use a metal baking dish or a loaf pan, which will fit inside your air fryer oven.
3. Place the container with the ice cream mixture in the freezer and freeze for at least 4 hours or until it becomes solid.
4. Once the ice cream is solid, remove it from the freezer and let it sit at room temperature for a few minutes to soften slightly. This will make it easier to scoop.
5. While the ice cream is softening, preheat your air fryer oven to 320°F (160°C).
6. Once the ice cream has softened, use a spoon or ice cream scoop to transfer it to a mixing bowl. Beat the ice cream with an electric mixer on low speed for about 1-2 minutes until it becomes creamy and smooth.
7. Transfer the whipped ice cream back to the freezer-safe container, smoothing the top with a spatula.
8. Place the container with the ice cream into the preheated air fryer oven.
9. Air fry the ice cream at 320°F (160°C) for about 10-12 minutes or until the top is lightly browned and the ice cream is warmed through. Keep an eye on it to avoid burning.
10. Once done, remove the container from the air fryer oven and let the ice cream cool for a few minutes before serving.

Nutrition per portion: Calories: 400 kcal, Fat: 34 g, Carbohydrates: 24g - Protein: 3g - Fiber: 0 g - Sugars: 23 g

Tip: Use a Stand Mixer for Ultra-Creamy Texture: When you remove the ice cream from the freezer to soften and whip it, use a stand mixer with a paddle attachment instead of a hand mixer. This method can help incorporate more air into the ice cream, resulting in a lighter, creamier texture. Whip on low to medium speed just until the ice cream becomes smooth and creamy. Avoid over-whipping to maintain the desired consistency.

97. AIR FRYER OVEN FRESH FRUIT TART

Prep: 15 min | **Cook time:** 15 min | **Serving:** 6-8

Ingredients:

» 1 pre-made or homemade pie crust (store-bought or follow your favorite pie crust recipe)

» 1 cup pastry cream or custard (you can make your own or buy it pre-made)

» Assorted fresh fruits (e.g., strawberries, blueberries, raspberries, kiwi, peaches, etc.)

Instructions:

1. Preheat your air fryer oven to the recommended temperature for baking, usually around 375°F (190°C).

2. Roll out the pie crust to fit the size of your air fryer oven basket or tray. Carefully place the rolled-out crust into the air fryer basket or tray, making sure it covers the bottom and sides.

3. Prick the bottom of the pie crust with a fork to prevent it from puffing up during baking.

4. Bake the pie crust in the preheated air fryer for about 8-10 minutes or until it becomes golden brown and fully cooked. Keep an eye on it as air fryers can cook faster than conventional ovens.

5. Remove the pie crust from the air fryer and let it cool completely.

6. Once the pie crust has cooled, spread a layer of pastry cream or custard evenly over the bottom of the crust.

7. Arrange the fresh fruit on top of the pastry cream in a decorative pattern.

8. Optional: You can glaze the fruit with a mixture of apricot jam or honey diluted with a little water to add shine and sweetness to the tart.

9. Serve the fresh fruit tart immediately or refrigerate until ready to serve.

Nutrition per portion: Calories: 270 kcal - Protein: 3g - Fat: 16g - Carbohydrates: 30g - Fiber: 2g - Sugars: 9g

Blind Bake with Pie Weights for an Even Crust: When baking the pie crust, use pie weights or dried beans to blind-bake it. After placing the crust in the air fryer basket or tray, line it with parchment paper and fill it with pie weights or dried beans. This will help prevent the crust from puffing up and ensure an even, flat base for your tart. Remove the weights and parchment paper halfway through baking to allow the crust to fully crisp up and turn golden brown.

Chill the Tart Before Serving for Better Slicing: Once you've assembled your tart with the pastry cream and fresh fruits, refrigerate it for at least 30 minutes before serving. This will help the pastry cream set and firm up, making it easier to slice the tart cleanly. Additionally, chilling the tart enhances the flavors and provides a refreshing contrast between the crispy crust and creamy filling.

FESTIVE DISHES

98. CROUTONS WITH GOAT CHEESE AND HONEY

Prep: 10 min | **Cook time:** 8-10 min | **Serving:** 4

Ingredients:

- » 4 cups of day-old bread cubes (such as baguette or ciabatta)
- » 4 oz goat cheese, crumbled
- » 2 tablespoons honey
- » 2 tablespoons olive oil
- » 1/2 teaspoon garlic powder
- » Salt and pepper to taste
- » Fresh thyme leaves for garnish (optional)

Instructions:

1. Preheat your air fryer oven to 375°F (190°C).
2. In a mixing bowl, combine the olive oil, honey, garlic powder, salt, and pepper.
3. Add the bread cubes to the bowl and toss them until they are evenly coated with the mixture.
4. Place the coated bread cubes in the air fryer basket, ensuring they are spread out in a single layer for even cooking.
5. Cook the bread cubes in the air fryer oven for 4-5 minutes until they become crispy and golden brown.
6. Open the air fryer oven and carefully sprinkle the crumbled goat cheese over the toasted bread cubes.
7. Place the basket back in the air fryer and cook for an additional 3-4 minutes or until the goat cheese softens and begins to melt.
8. Once done, remove the croutons from the air fryer and let them cool for a minute or two.
9. Garnish with fresh thyme leaves if desired.
10. Serve the Croutons with Goat Cheese and Honey as a delightful side dish or snack.

Nutrition per portion: Calories: 250 kcal, Carbohydrates: 25g, Protein: 8g, Fat: 14g, Fiber: 1g – Sugars: 10 g

Ensure Even Coating and Cooking: To ensure that the bread cubes are evenly coated with the olive oil, honey, and seasoning mixture, you can use a large ziplock bag. Add the bread cubes and the oil mixture to the bag, seal it, and shake it well until the bread cubes are evenly coated. This method also helps in achieving a uniform golden-brown color when air frying. Additionally, shake the air fryer basket halfway through the initial cooking time to ensure all sides of the croutons get crispy.

99. SMOKED SALMON AND AVOCADO CANAPÉS

Prep: 15 min | **Cook time:** 5 min | **Serving:** 4

Ingredients:

» 8 slices of baguette or small bread rounds
» 1 ripe avocado, peeled and sliced
» 4 ounces smoked salmon, thinly sliced
» 2 tablespoons cream cheese
» 1 tablespoon fresh dill, chopped
» 1 teaspoon lemon juice
» Salt and pepper to taste
» Olive oil spray (for the air fryer)

Instructions:

1. Preheat your air fryer oven to 375°F (190°C).
2. In a small bowl, mix the cream cheese, chopped dill, lemon juice, salt, and pepper.
3. Lay out the baguette slices or bread rounds on a clean surface. Lightly toast them if desired.
4. Spread a thin layer of the cream cheese mixture onto each slice of bread.
5. Top each canapé with a slice of smoked salmon and a few slices of avocado.
6. Place the canapés in a single layer in the air fryer basket. You may need to work in batches depending on the size of your air fryer.
7. Lightly spray the canapés with olive oil to help them brown and crisp up.
8. Air fry the canapés at 375°F (190°C) for about 5 minutes or until the bread is crispy and the salmon is slightly warmed.
9. Remove the canapés from the air fryer and arrange them on a serving platter.
10. Garnish with additional fresh dill if desired and serve immediately.

Nutrition per portion: Calories: 200 kcal, Total Fat: 12g, Carbohydrates: 17g, Sugars: 1g, Protein: 8g – Fiber: 2 g – Sugars: 1 g

Prevent Avocado from Browning: To keep the avocado slices looking fresh and vibrant, toss them in a little extra lemon juice before assembling the canapés. This will prevent the avocado from browning while adding a nice tangy flavor that complements the smoked salmon and cream cheese mixture.

Ensure Even Crispness of the Bread: For evenly crispy bread, lightly toast the baguette slices or bread rounds in the air fryer before adding the toppings. Spray the bread with a bit of olive oil and air fry at 375°F (190°C) for 2-3 minutes until they are just starting to crisp up. This pre-toasting step ensures that the bread remains crispy even after adding the cream cheese, salmon, and avocado, giving you a delightful crunch with every bite.

100. AIR FRYER HAM AND CHEESE PUFFS

Prep: 15 min | **Cook time:** 15 min | **Serving:** 12 puffs

Ingredients:

- » 1 sheet of puff pastry, thawed
- » 6-8 slices of ham
- » 1 cup shredded cheese (cheddar, mozzarella, or your favorite cheese)
- » 1 egg, beaten (for egg wash)
- » Optional: Dijon mustard or any other sauce for dipping

Instructions:

1. Preheat your air fryer oven to 375°F (190°C).
2. Roll out the thawed puff pastry sheet on a lightly floured surface.
3. Cut the pastry sheet into small squares, approximately 3x3 inches.
4. Place a slice of ham and a tablespoon of shredded cheese in the center of each square.
5. Fold the pastry over the ham and cheese, forming a triangle, and press the edges firmly to seal. You can use a fork to create a decorative edge.
6. Place the filled puffs on a baking sheet or in the air fryer basket, leaving some space between each puff.
7. Brush the puffs with the beaten egg to give them a golden and glossy finish.
8. Place the baking sheet or air fryer basket into the preheated air fryer oven.
9. Air fry the ham and cheese puffs at 375°F (190°C) for 10-15 minutes or until they become golden brown and puffy.
10. Once done, remove the puffs from the air fryer and let them cool for a minute or two before serving.
11. Serve the puffs warm with Dijon mustard or any other sauce of your choice for dipping.

Nutrition per portion: Calories: 170 kcal - Fat: 12 g - Carbohydrates: 12 g, Protein: 6 g – Fiber: 0 g - Sugars: 0 g -

Ensure Proper Sealing for Puff Pastry: To prevent the filling from leaking out during cooking, ensure the puff pastry edges are tightly sealed. Press firmly along the edges of each triangle to seal them securely. You can also use a fork to crimp the edges for an extra seal. This will help the puffs maintain their shape and prevent any cheese from oozing out while they cook.

101. AIR FRYER OVEN MEATBALLS WITH MUSHROOM SAUCE

Prep: 15 min | **Cook time:** 15 min | **Serving:** 4

Ingredients:

- » For Meatballs:
- » 1 pound ground beef (or a mix of beef and pork)
- » 1/2 cup breadcrumbs
- » 1/4 cup grated Parmesan cheese
- » 1/4 cup milk
- » 1 large egg
- » 2 cloves garlic, minced
- » 1 teaspoon dried oregano
- » 1 teaspoon dried basil

- » 1/2 teaspoon salt
- » 1/4 teaspoon black pepper
- » For Mushroom Sauce:
- » 2 cups sliced mushrooms (button or cremini)
- » 1 tablespoon olive oil
- » 1 cup beef broth
- » 1 cup heavy cream
- » 2 tablespoons all-purpose flour
- » Salt and pepper to taste
- » Fresh parsley for garnish (optional)

Instructions:

1. Preheat your air fryer oven to 375°F (190°C).
2. In a large mixing bowl, combine all the meatball ingredients: ground beef, breadcrumbs, grated Parmesan cheese, milk, egg, minced garlic, dried oregano, dried basil, salt, and black pepper. Mix well until all ingredients are evenly incorporated.
3. Shape the mixture into 1-inch meatballs and place them on a greased or parchment paper-lined air fryer oven tray.
4. Cook the meatballs in the preheated air fryer oven for about 12-15 minutes or until they are fully cooked and nicely browned. You may need to do this in batches depending on the size of your air fryer oven.
5. While the meatballs are cooking, prepare the mushroom sauce. In a saucepan, heat the olive oil over medium heat. Add the sliced mushrooms and sauté until they are tender and lightly browned.
6. In a separate bowl, whisk together the beef broth, heavy cream, and all-purpose flour until there are no lumps.
7. Pour the broth and cream mixture into the saucepan with the sautéed mushrooms. Stir continuously until the sauce thickens and coats the back of a spoon. Season with salt and pepper to taste.
8. Once the meatballs are done, serve them with the mushroom sauce drizzled on top. Garnish with fresh parsley if desired.

Nutrition per portion: Calories: 475 kcal, Protein: 28 g - Fat: 33 g, Carbohydrates: 16 g – Fiber: 2 g – Sugars: 3 g

102. ARANCINI PASTA WITH MEAT SAUCE AND PEAS

Prep: 20 min | **Cook time:** 25 min | **Serving:** 4

Ingredients:

» 2 cups cooked pasta (such as penne or rigatoni)
» 1 cup cooked ground meat (beef, pork, or a combination)
» 1/2 cup frozen peas, thawed
» 1/2 cup grated Parmesan cheese
» 2 large eggs, beaten
» 1 cup breadcrumbs
» 1/2 teaspoon salt
» 1/4 teaspoon black pepper
» 1/2 teaspoon dried oregano
» 1/2 teaspoon garlic powder
» 1/4 teaspoon red pepper flakes (optional)
» Cooking spray or olive oil spray
» For the meat sauce:
» 1 cup tomato sauce
» 1 tablespoon olive oil
» 1 small onion, finely chopped
» 2 garlic cloves, minced
» 1/2 teaspoon dried basil
» 1/2 teaspoon dried oregano
» Salt and pepper to taste

Instructions:

1. In a medium-sized bowl, combine the cooked pasta, cooked ground meat, thawed peas, grated Parmesan cheese, beaten eggs, salt, black pepper, dried oregano, garlic powder, and red pepper flakes (if using). Mix well until all ingredients are evenly distributed.
2. Preheat your air fryer oven to 375°F (190°C).
3. Prepare the meat sauce: In a saucepan, heat the olive oil over medium heat. Add the chopped onion and minced garlic, and sauté until they become translucent. Stir in the tomato sauce, dried basil, dried oregano, salt, and pepper. Let the sauce simmer for about 5-10 minutes to allow the flavors to meld together.
4. Take about 2 tablespoons of the pasta mixture and shape it into a ball. Repeat until all the mixture is used. You should get around 16-20 arancini balls, depending on the size.
5. Roll each arancini ball in the breadcrumbs, making sure they are coated evenly.
6. Lightly spray the air fryer basket with cooking spray or olive oil spray to prevent sticking. Place the arancini balls in the basket, leaving space between them for even cooking. You may need to cook them in batches depending on the size of your air fryer oven.
7. Air fry the arancini balls at 375°F (190°C) for about 10-12 minutes, flipping them halfway through the cooking time for even browning.
8. While the arancini balls are cooking, reheat the meat sauce if needed.
9. Once the arancini balls are crispy and golden brown, remove them from the air fryer oven and serve them hot with the meat sauce.

Nutrition per portion: Calories: 480 kcal - Protein: 28 g - Fat: 18 g Carbohydrates: 52 g – Fiber: 5 g – Sugars: 5 g

103. SALMON MOUSSE WITH SPRING ONION

Prep: 15 min | **Cook time:** 10 min | **Serving:** 4

Ingredients:

- » 1 lb (450g) fresh salmon fillet, skinless and boneless
- » 1/2 cup cream cheese
- » 1/4 cup mayonnaise
- » 1/4 cup chopped spring onions (scallions)
- » 1 tablespoon lemon juice
- » 1 teaspoon Dijon mustard
- » 1 teaspoon fresh dill, chopped
- » Salt and pepper to taste
- » Cooking spray or oil for greasing

Instructions:

1. Preheat your Air Fryer Oven to 375°F (190°C).
2. Cut the salmon into small chunks and place them in a food processor. Pulse until the salmon is finely chopped and forms a smooth paste.
3. In a mixing bowl, combine the salmon paste, cream cheese, mayonnaise, chopped spring onions, lemon juice, Dijon mustard, and chopped dill. Mix well until all ingredients are evenly combined.
4. Season the mixture with salt and pepper to taste. Adjust the seasoning according to your preference.
5. Lightly grease small ramekins or oven-safe dishes with cooking spray or oil.
6. Divide the salmon mousse mixture evenly among the ramekins.
7. Place the ramekins in the Air Fryer Oven basket, ensuring they are not touching each other.
8. Air fry the salmon mousse at 375°F (190°C) for about 10 minutes or until the top is slightly golden and the mousse is set.
9. Once done, carefully remove the ramekins from the Air Fryer Oven and let them cool for a few minutes before serving.

Nutrition per portion: Calories: 318 kcal - Protein: 22g - Fat: 24g - Carbohydrates: 4g - Fiber: 0g - Sugars: 2g

Enhance Flavor with Marination: Before processing the salmon, consider marinating it for added flavor. Mix together some lemon juice, olive oil, garlic, and herbs like dill or parsley in a bowl. Coat the salmon chunks with this mixture and let them marinate in the refrigerator for at least 30 minutes before processing. Marinating the salmon adds depth of flavor and ensures a more aromatic and flavorful salmon mousse.

104. GNOCCHI WITH GORGONZOLA AND WALNUTS

Prep: 10 min | **Cook time:** 15 min | **Serving:** 4

Ingredients:

- » 1 lb (450g) store-bought gnocchi
- » 2 tbsp olive oil
- » 1/2 cup crumbled Gorgonzola cheese
- » 1/4 cup chopped walnuts
- » 1/4 cup chopped fresh parsley (optional, for garnish)
- » Salt and pepper, to taste

Instructions:

1. Preheat your air fryer oven to 400°F (200°C).
2. In a large mixing bowl, toss the gnocchi with olive oil until evenly coated.
3. Spread the gnocchi in a single layer on the air fryer oven basket or tray.
4. Place the basket or tray into the preheated air fryer oven and cook for about 12-15 minutes, shaking or stirring the gnocchi halfway through to ensure even cooking. The gnocchi should be golden and slightly crispy.
5. While the gnocchi is cooking, prepare the sauce. In a small saucepan over low heat, melt the Gorgonzola cheese until it becomes creamy and smooth.
6. Once the gnocchi is done cooking, remove it from the air fryer oven and transfer it to a serving dish.
7. Pour the melted Gorgonzola cheese over the gnocchi and toss gently to coat.
8. Sprinkle the chopped walnuts on top of the gnocchi.
9. Garnish with chopped parsley if desired.
10. Serve immediately and enjoy your delicious Air Fryer Oven Gnocchi with Gorgonzola and Walnuts!

Nutrition per portion: Calories: 430 kcal - Carbohydrates: 38g - Protein: 11g - Fat: 27g – Fiber: 2 g - Sugar: 2g

Ensure Even Coating: When tossing the gnocchi with olive oil in the mixing bowl, make sure each piece is evenly coated. This ensures that they cook uniformly and develop a golden, crispy exterior in the air fryer oven.

105. POTATO AND SAUSAGE FLAN

Prep: 20 min **Cook time:** 15 min | **Serving:** 4

Ingredients:

» 2 large potatoes, peeled and thinly sliced
» 1 lb (450g) sausage (pork, chicken, or turkey), sliced
» 1 medium onion, finely chopped
» 1 red bell pepper, diced
» 1 green bell pepper, diced

» 4 large eggs
» 1 cup milk
» 1 cup shredded cheddar cheese
» 1 tablespoon olive oil
» Salt and pepper to taste
» Cooking spray (for greasing the air fryer basket)

Instructions:

1. Preheat your air fryer oven to 375°F (190°C).
2. In a large skillet, heat the olive oil over medium heat. Add the chopped onions and cook until they become translucent.
3. Add the sliced sausages to the skillet and cook until they are browned and fully cooked. Then, add the diced bell peppers and continue cooking for a few more minutes until the peppers soften. Season with salt and pepper to taste. Set aside.
4. In a separate bowl, whisk the eggs and milk together until well combined. Stir in half of the shredded cheddar cheese.
5. Grease the air fryer basket with cooking spray to prevent sticking.
6. Layer half of the thinly sliced potatoes in the greased air fryer basket, slightly overlapping each other. Spread half of the sausage and pepper mixture on top of the potatoes.
7. Pour half of the egg and cheese mixture over the potato and sausage layer, ensuring it is evenly distributed.
8. Repeat the layering process with the remaining potatoes, sausage mixture, and egg mixture.
9. Sprinkle the remaining shredded cheddar cheese on top.
10. Place the air fryer basket in the preheated air fryer oven and cook at 375°F (190°C) for about 25 minutes or until the flan is set and the top is golden brown.

Nutrition per portion: Calories: 375 kcal - Protein: 18 g - Carbohydrates: 18 g -Fat: 18 g - Fiber: 3 g- Sugars: 2 g

CLASSIC 28-MEAL PLAN

Week 1:

DAY	BREAKFAST	LUNCH	DINNER	SNACK
Monday	Banana Pancakes	Grilled Chicken with Barbecue Sauce	Quinoa and Lentil Burger	Stuffed Artichokes
Tuesday	Apple and Cinnamon Muffins	Sesame tofu	Baked Stuffed Mushrooms Air Fryer	Ham and Mozzarella Cheese Sandwich
Wednesday	Bacon and Cheese Omelet	Vegetable Casserole	Beef Filet with Green Pepper	Tuna and Sun-Dried Tomato Sandwich
Thursday	Oatmeal and honey pancakes	Potato and Spinach Croquettes	Roast of Beef with Potatoes	Chicken and Avocado Sandwich
Friday	Waffles with Maple Syrup	Baked Salmon with Lemon And Herbs	Skewers of Beef and Vegetables	Focaccia with Cherry Tomatoes and Basil
Saturday	Nutella Crepes	Vegetarian Lasagna with Spinach and Ricotta Cheese	Pork Tenderloin in Bacon Crust	Pizza Margherita
Sunday	Banana and Chocolate Porridge	Porcini Mushroom Risotto	Chicken Curry	Eggplant and Goat Cheese Sandwich

Week 2:

DAY	BREAKFAST	LUNCH	DINNER	SNACK
Monday	French Toast	Chickpea and Sweet Potato Meatballs	Beef Stew With Vegetables	Tuna and Sun-Dried Tomato Sandwich
Tuesday	Omelet with Spinach and Cheese	Vegetarian Chili with Beans and Corn	Lamb Costolets	Ham and Mozzarella Cheese Sandwich
Wednesday	Banana and Oatmeal Cheese Pancakes	Vegetarian Lasagna with Spinach and Ricotta Cheese	Sliced Beef with Rocket and Grana Cheese	Chicken and Avocado Sandwich
Thursday	Bruschette with Sun-Dried Tomatoes and Mozzarella Cheese	Porcini Mushroom Risotto	Pineapple Cod Fillets	Stuffed Artichokes
Friday	Olive all'ascolana	Porcini Mushroom Risotto	Pineapple Squid	Focaccia with Cherry Tomatoes and Basil
Saturday	Crostini with Liver Pate	Grilled Vegetable Tacos	Pineapple Coconut Shrimp	Pizza Margherita
Sunday	Pinzimonio with Fresh Vegetables and Yogurt Sauce	Potato and Spinach Croquettes	Pineapple Chicken Wings	Eggplant and Goat Cheese Sandwich

Week 3:

DAY	BREAKFAST	LUNCH	DINNER	SNACK
Monday	Bacon and Cheese Omelet	Grilled Chicken with Grilled Vegetables	Beef Hamburger with Bacon and Cheese	Stuffed Artichokes
Tuesday	French Toast	Baked Stuffed Mushrooms Air Fryer	Roast of lamb with rosemary and garlic	Ham and Mozzarella Cheese Sandwich
Wednesday	Omelet with Spinach and Cheese	Vegetable Casserole	Pizzaiola Meat	Tuna and Sun-Dried Tomato Sandwich
Thursday	Banana and Oatmeal Cheese Pancakes	Chickpea and Sweet Potato Meatballs	Beef Stew With Vegetables	Chicken and Avocado Sandwich
Friday	Waffles with Maple Syrup	Sesame tofu	Lamb Stew with Carrots and Peas	Focaccia with Cherry Tomatoes and Basil
Saturday	Nutella Crepes	Vegetarian Lasagna with Spinach and Ricotta Cheese	Pork Stew with Mushrooms and Potatoes	Pizza Margherita
Sunday	Banana and Chocolate Porridge	Porcini Mushroom Risotto	Pork Ribs with Tomato Salad	Eggplant and Goat Cheese Sandwich

Week 4:

DAY	BREAKFAST	LUNCH	DINNER	SNACK
Monday	French Toast	Baked Stuffed Mushrooms Air Fryer	Chicken Hunting	Stuffed Artichokes
Tuesday	Banana Pancakes	Vegetable Casserole	Chicken's Breast With Lemon	Tuna and Sun-Dried Tomato Sandwich
Wednesday	Bacon and Cheese Omelet	Quinoa and Lentil Burger	Roasted Chicken With Potatoes	Chicken and Avocado Sandwich
Thursday	Oatmeal and honey pancakes	Potato and Spinach Croquettes	Chicken Curry	Focaccia with Cherry Tomatoes and Basil
Friday	Waffles with Maple Syrup	Sesame tofu	Spicy Chicken Wings	Pizza Margherita
Saturday	Nutella Crepes	Grilled Vegetable Tacos	Baked Chicken With Spices	Ham and Mozzarella Cheese Sandwich
Sunday	Banana and Chocolate Porridge	Porcini Mushroom Risotto	Pork Roast with Potatoes	Eggplant and Goat Cheese Sandwich

LOW-CALORIE 28-MEAL PLAN

Week 1:

DAY	BREAKFAST	LUNCH	DINNER	SNACK
Monday	Banana Pancakes	Grilled Chicken with Barbecue Sauce	Quinoa and Lentil Burger	Stuffed Artichokes
Tuesday	Apple and Cinnamon Muffins	Sesame tofu	Baked Stuffed Mushrooms Air Fryer	Ham and Mozzarella Cheese Sandwich
Wednesday	Bacon and Cheese Omelet	Vegetable Casserole	Beef Filet with Green Pepper	Tuna and Sun-Dried Tomato Sandwich
Thursday	Oatmeal and Honey Pancakes	Potato and Spinach Croquettes	Roast of Beef with Potatoes	Chicken and Avocado Sandwich
Friday	Waffles with Maple Syrup	Baked Salmon with Lemon And Herbs	Skewers of Beef and Vegetables	Focaccia with Cherry Tomatoes and Basil
Saturday	Nutella Crepes	Vegetarian Lasagna with Spinach and Ricotta Cheese	Pork Tenderloin in Bacon Crust	Pizza Margherita
Sunday	Banana and Chocolate Porridge	Porcini Mushroom Risotto	Chicken Curry	Eggplant and Goat Cheese Sandwich

Week 2:

DAY	BREAKFAST	LUNCH	DINNER	SNACK
Monday	French Toast	Chickpea and Sweet Potato Meatballs	Beef Stew With Vegetables	Tuna and Sun-Dried Tomato Sandwich
Tuesday	Omelet with Spinach and Cheese	Vegetarian Chili with Beans and Corn	Lamb Costolets	Ham and Mozzarella Cheese Sandwich
Wednesday	Banana and Oatmeal Cheese Pancakes	Vegetarian Lasagna with Spinach and Ricotta Cheese	Sliced Beef with Rocket and Grana Cheese	Chicken and Avocado Sandwich
Thursday	Bruschette with Sun-Dried Tomatoes and Mozzarella Cheese	Porcini Mushroom Risotto	Pineapple Cod Fillets	Stuffed Artichokes
Friday	Olive all'ascolana	Porcini Mushroom Risotto	Pineapple Squid	Focaccia with Cherry Tomatoes and Basil
Saturday	Crostini with Liver Pate	Grilled Vegetable Tacos	Pineapple Coconut Shrimp	Pizza Margherita
Sunday	Pinzimonio with Fresh Vegetables and Yogurt Sauce	Potato and Spinach Croquettes	Pineapple Chicken Wings	Eggplant and Goat Cheese Sandwich

Week 3:

DAY	BREAKFAST	LUNCH	DINNER	SNACK
Monday	Bacon and Cheese Omelet	Grilled Chicken with Grilled Vegetables	Beef Hamburger with Bacon and Cheese	Stuffed Artichokes
Tuesday	French Toast	Baked Stuffed Mushrooms Air Fryer	Roast of Lamb with Rosemary and Garlic	Ham and Mozzarella Cheese Sandwich
Wednesday	Omelet with Spinach and Cheese	Vegetable Casserole	Pizzaiola Meat	Tuna and Sun-Dried Tomato Sandwich
Thursday	Banana and Oatmeal Cheese Pancakes	Chickpea and Sweet Potato Meatballs	Beef Stew With Vegetables	Chicken and Avocado Sandwich
Friday	Waffles with Maple Syrup	Sesame tofu	Lamb Stew with Carrots and Peas	Focaccia with Cherry Tomatoes and Basil
Saturday	Nutella Crepes	Vegetarian Lasagna with Spinach and Ricotta Cheese	Pork Stew with Mushrooms and Potatoes	Pizza Margherita
Sunday	Banana and Chocolate Porridge	Porcini Mushroom Risotto	Pork Ribs with Tomato Salad	Eggplant and Goat Cheese Sandwich

Week 4:

DAY	BREAKFAST	LUNCH	DINNER	SNACK
Monday	French Toast	Baked Stuffed Mushrooms Air Fryer	Chicken Hunting	Stuffed Artichokes
Tuesday	Banana Pancakes	Vegetable Casserole	Chicken's Breast With Lemon	Tuna and Sun-Dried Tomato Sandwich
Wednesday	Bacon and Cheese Omelet	Quinoa and Lentil Burger	Roasted Chicken With Potatoes	Chicken and Avocado Sandwich
Thursday	Oatmeal and Honey Pancakes	Potato and Spinach Croquettes	Chicken Curry	Focaccia with Cherry Tomatoes and Basil
Friday	Waffles with Maple Syrup	Sesame tofu	Spicy Chicken Wings	Pizza Margherita
Saturday	Nutella Crepes	Grilled Vegetable Tacos	Baked Chicken With Spices	Ham and Mozzarella Cheese Sandwich
Sunday	Banana and Chocolate Porridge	Porcini Mushroom Risotto	Pork Roast with Potatoes	Eggplant and Goat Cheese Sandwich

CONCLUSION

If you plan to purchase the Breville Smart Air Fryer Oven Pro, then this cookbook is a perfect choice. I hope you will understand all the features and cooking methods of this appliance. You can prepare recipes from this book with Breville Smart Air Fryer Oven Pro. You didn't need to buy a separate appliance or dehydrator to bake or dehydrate food. You will get delicious, healthy, easy-to-prepare, and quick recipes from this cookbook. My cookbook has different chapters that contain details about this kitchen appliance. You don't need another appliance because it has all-in-one cooking functions. You can prepare your favorite foods on different occasions with this appliance. You can prepare a quick breakfast in the morning for your kids. If you choose my cookbook, your choice is best because we added all information about appliances. This appliance offers all the useful functions that you need. I added delicious recipes for your Ninja Foodi Digital air fryer oven cooking appliance. Select, read, and start cooking. I hope you will love this cookbook. If you don't have any knowledge of using this appliance, read this cookbook thoroughly. I hope you will get all the answers that come to your mind. Thank you for appreciating us for purchasing this cookbook. Thank you for purchasing my cookbook. Thank you, good luck!

Thank you for exploring our recipe book! If you enjoyed our recipes and found them helpful, we'd greatly appreciate it if you could take a moment to leave a review. Your feedback is invaluable to us and helps other food enthusiasts discover our book. Happy cooking, and we look forward to hearing about your culinary adventures!

Dear reader,

I'm delighted that you've reached the last page of our recipe book! I would like to sincerely thank you for taking the time to explore our delicious culinary creations. I hope you found inspiration and enjoyment in reading the recipes.

If you're satisfied with the book and would like to share your experience, I would be extremely grateful if you could leave a review on Amazon. Your feedback is essential to us and helps us improve.

BONUS

THANK YOU FOR PURCHASING OUR RECIPE BOOK!

To enhance your culinary experience, we have included a special bonus just for you. Download the full-color PDF version of our recipe book, complete with high-resolution photos of every dish, by scanning the QR code below or visiting

https://drive.google.com/drive/folders/15WdXwoyU_zJ3keyKpI8fSgOTYPY3ZVrG?usp=sharing

For any information or clarification, please feel free to contact us at the email address
semplicesavor@gmail.com

Thank you again for your support and happy cooking!

Best regards,

SEMPLICESAVOR

INDEX

A

Air Fryer Ham and Cheese Puffs	112
Air Fryer Lemon Doughnut	101
Air Fryer Oven Apple and Cinnamon Crumble	106
Air Fryer Oven Banana and Chocolate Muffins	104
Air Fryer Oven Catalan Cream with Caramel	105
Air Fryer Oven Chocolate and Hazelnut Cake	107
Air Fryer Oven Chocolate Cheesecake	100
Air Fryer Oven Dark Chocolate Brownies	103
Air Fryer Oven Fresh Fruit Tart	109
Air Fryer Oven Homemade Vanilla Ice Cream	108
Air Fryer Oven Meatballs with Mushroom Sauce	113
Air Fryer Oven Strawberry Tiramisu	98
Apple and Cinnamon Muffins	11
Arancini Pasta with Meat Sauce and Peas	115
Arancini with Meat Sauce	26
Artichokes Stuffed	79

B

Bacon and Cheese Omelet	12
Baked Chicken With Spices	48
Baked Potato Chips	25
Baked Salmon with Lemon And Herbs	40
Baked Stuffed Mushrooms Air Fryer	78
Banana and Chocolate Porridge	16
Banana and Oatmeal Cheese Pancakes	19
Banana Pancakes	10
Bananas Falafel	39
Beef Filet With Green Pepper	51
Beef Hamburger with Bacon and Cheese	59
Beef Stew With Vegetables	55
Bruschette with Sun-Dried Tomatoes and Mozzarella Cheese	20

C

Calzone with Ham and Cheese	94
Chicken and Avocado Sandwich	89
Chicken Curry	44
Chicken Hunting	41
Chicken's Breast With Lemon	42
Chicken Straccetti with Rucola And Tomatoes	47
Chicken With Mushrooms And Panna	50
Chickpea and Sweet Potato Meatballs	81
Crostini with Liver Pate	22

Croutons with Goat Cheese and Honey	110

E

Eggplant and Goat Cheese Sandwich	92

F

Focaccia with Cherry Tomatoes and Basil	90
French Toast	17

G

Gnocchi with Gorgonzola and Walnuts	118
Grilled Chicken With Barbecue Sauce	46
Grilled Chicken With Grilled Vegetables	49
Grilled Vegetable Tacos	74

H

Ham and Mozzarella Cheese Sandwich	87

K

Kale chips	80

L

Lamb Costolets	56
Lamb Stew with Carrots And Peas	60

M

Mini Quiche with Spinach and Cheese	27

N

Nutella Crepes	15

O

Oatmeal and honey pancakes	13
Olive all'ascolana	21
Omelet with Spinach and Cheese	18

P

Pigeon Bread with Carrots and Sedanes 66
Pineapple Air Fryer Fried Ravioli 38
Pineapple Chicken Wings 34
Pineapple Coconut Shrimp 32
Pineapple Cod Fillets 30
Pineapple Corn Fritters 37
Pineapple Squid 31
Pineapple Sweet Potato Fries 36
Pineapple Tuna Meatballs 33
Pinzimonio with Fresh Vegetables and Yogurt Sauce 23
Pizzaiola Meat 58
Pizza Margherita 91
Pizza with Mushrooms and Sausage 93
Porcini Mushroom Risotto 85
Pork Curry with Based Rice 67
Pork Pulpets with Sugar 73
Pork Ribs 62
Pork Ribs with Tomato Salad 70
Pork Roast with Potatoes 61
Pork Sausages 72
Pork Slices with Senape 71
Pork Stew with Mushrooms And Potatoes 65
Pork Tenderloin in Bacon Crust 63
Potato and Cheese Croquettes 29
Potato and Sausage Flan 119
Potato and Spinach Croquettes 77

Q

Quinoa and Lentil Burger 84

R

Roasted Chicken With Potatoes 43
Roast Of Beef With Potatoes 52

Roast of lamb with rosemary and garlic 57
Roast Pork with Potatoes and Carrots 68

S

Salmon and Arugula Pizza 95
Salmon Mousse with Spring Onion 117
Sandwich with Meatballs and Tomato Sauce 96
Savory Pie with Zucchini and Carrots 86
Sea Bass in Pineapple Air Fryer 35
Sesame tofu 75
Shrimp and Pineapple Skewers 28
Skewers of Beef and Vegetables 53
Skewers of Pigs and Pineapples 64
Sliced Beef with Rocket and Grana Cheese 54
Smoked Salmon and Avocado Canapés 111
Spicy Chicken Wings 45
Stewed Pig with Beans 69

T

Tuna and Potato Meatballs 24
Tuna and Sun-Dried Tomato Sandwich 88

V

Vegetable Casserole 76
Vegetarian Chili with Beans and Corn 82
Vegetarian Lasagna with Spinach and Ricotta Cheese 83

W

Waffles with Maple Syrup 14

Made in United States
Orlando, FL
24 November 2024

54382187R10070